praise for john schlimm

PRAISE FOR *THE CHEESY VEGAN*:

"The Cheesy Vegan proves the point that living a vegan lifestyle doesn't mean giving up your favorite foods. These recipes are good for the body and leave nothing to be desired—John Schlimm is the Bobby Flay of the vegan movement."

—Eddy Lu, CEO and co-founder of Grubwithus

"With The Cheesy Vegan, John Schlimm continues his unique brand of tasty activism. Once again, John uses an irresistible and family-friendly collection of plant-based dishes that everyone, vegan and carnivore alike, will devour to poignantly convey his unconditional love for all animals."

—Robin Ganzert, PhD, president and CEO of American Humane Association

"The Cheesy Vegan is a heavenly dose of cheese-filled recipes that will please any and every palate. Take one look at the mouth-watering photos and recipes and you'll want to dive right in (to a pool of vegan cheesecake)!"

—Christy Morgan, The Blissful Chef, author of *Blissful Bites: Vegan Meals That Nourish Mind, Body, and Planet*

"It's hard to count the number of people who've told me over the years, 'I could never stop eating cheese!' Well, John Schlimm is here to say you don't have to! In The Cheesy Vegan, he's got a plethora of homemade vegan cheeses and related recipes that you're sure to love, and cows will love you for choosing them!"

—Paul Shapiro, vice president of Farm Animal Protection for The Humane Society of the United States and founder of Compassion Over Killing

"John's recipes are my go-to for inspiration and The Cheesy Vegan is no exception. He's actually come up with the missing link to making vegan eating complete—a great tasting and easy recipe for vegan blue cheese. Don't be surprised if you see that one on our menu!"

—Doron Petersan, founder of Sticky Fingers Sweets & Eats and author of *Sticky Fingers' Sweets*

"The homemade vegan cheeses and other related recipes in this beautifully crafted book bring health and kindness to a luscious new level. Cheese was always the hardest for vegans to emulate, and the one thing most non-vegans crave the most, so with the publication of this new masterpiece, we see the handwriting on the wall: Veganville is getting closer every day. Highly recommended!"

—Will Tuttle, PhD, best-selling author of *The World Peace Diet*, recipient of the Courage of Conscience Award, co-founder of Veganpalooza and Circle of Compassion, and acclaimed pianist and composer

"Cheese is one of life's great treats and to have it when it's 'cruelty-free' is the best thing for all! John . . . Thank you for making the world a tastier place with The Cheesy Vegan!!!"

—Cornelia Guest, designer, philanthropist, and author of *Cornelia Guest's Simple Pleasures*

"For the past 26 years, I have been on exactly the same pathway as John Schlimm. I have wanted to delight and do less harm . . . and to have fun doing that. I literally am a kindred spirit except for one small thing: He is at least one lap ahead of me in being vegan. I'm so convinced about the power of plant-based foods in my own life and work that it is high time for me to take a deep breath and plunge into The Cheesy Vegan and see if I can at least not fall further behind! Let's join John—it seems to be a great way to enjoy the truly good life!"

—Graham Kerr, award-winning cookbook author, culinary consultant, and host of *The Galloping Gourmet*

PRAISE FOR *GRILLING VEGAN STYLE*:

"Our love for John Schlimm knows no bounds.... The man knows his way around a theme, not to mention a barbecue.... Schlimm is an author we'd love to stand around the grill with—gabbing, drinking, and saving the world all at once."

—VegNews

"A common-sense and fun book about grilling that even carnivores can enjoy."

—Washington Post

"Who knew you could have so much fun grilling everything from salads and sandwiches to desserts?! Grilling Vegan Style is more than a cookbook; it's a go-to handbook for outdoor living, eating, and celebrating."

—Rory Freedman, coauthor of the #1 *New York Times* best seller *Skinny Bitch*

"With Grilling Vegan Style, John has shown you ways to bring out flavors and taste you never thought possible. John's recipe for Party on South Peach Salsa especially is to die for and will go with almost anything."

—Chef Paul Kirk, CWC, PhD, BSAS, Kansas City Baron of BBQ, and author of *Championship Barbecue* and *America's Best BBQ*

"I have to admit that I was a little skeptical about a vegan grilling book. After all in my world it's all about the meat. I might even be considered a nonvegan! But John's book has opened my eyes to the concept and his recipes are outstanding."

—Ray Lampe a.k.a. Dr. BBQ, author of *Ribs, Chops, Steaks, and Wings* and *Dr. BBQ's Big-Time Barbecue Cookbook*

"Veggie backyard BBQ warriors and grill pan guerrillas; John Schlimm, your knight in tofu armor has arrived, also bearing Spiked Ruby Daiquiris and other sipping delights."

—Terry Hope Romero, author of *Viva Vegan!* and coauthor of *Veganomicon*

"This cookbook ensures that the magic of a summer barbecue or a night around the campfire can ignite your taste buds all year long."

—FoxNews.com

PRAISE FOR *THE TIPSY VEGAN*:

"His recipes are often spot-on and don't require too many arcane or hard-to-source ingredients. Moreover, the addition of alcohol to his dishes—Bottom's Up VegeBean Stew employs a dark beer for added oomph, Triple Sec is added to a blueberry pie as well as homemade granola—truly serves a purpose other than novelty.... Schlimm's efforts will pay off for vegans, as well as their omnivorous guests."

—Publishers Weekly

"With beautiful, vivid photography and a refreshingly lucid tone despite the focus on spirits, The Tipsy Vegan is already a winner, but with a cookbook, no matter how fun the novelty, the recipes are what it's all about, of course. This cookbook does not disappoint. An efficient but muscular little book, the recipes featured here are largely variations on classics but full of fun, flavor, and spark."

—Examiner.com

THE
CHEESY
VEGAN

other books by john schlimm:

Grilling Vegan Style

The Tipsy Vegan

Stand Up!

Twang: a novel

The Seven Stars Cookbook

The Ultimate Beer Lover's Cookbook

The Beer Lover's Cookbook

The Pennsylvania Celebrities Cookbook

Straub Brewery

The Straub Beer Party Drinks Handbook

The Straub Beer Cookbook

Corresponding with History

THE CHEESY VEGAN

More Than 125 Plant-Based Recipes for Indulging in the World's Ultimate Comfort Food

JOHN SCHLIMM

PHOTOGRAPHS BY AMY BEADLE ROTH

Da Capo
LIFE
LONG

A Member of the Perseus Books Group

Designed by Megan Jones Design (www.meganjonesdesign.com)
Set in 9 point Neutraface Light by Megan Jones Design

Library of Congress Cataloging-in-Publication Data
Schlimm, John E., 1971–
The cheesy vegan : more than 125 plant-based recipes for indulging in the world's ultimate comfort food /
John Schlimm ; photographs by Amy Beadle Roth.
pages cm
Includes index.
ISBN 978-0-7382-1679-9 (paperback)—ISBN 978-0-7382-1680-5 (e-book) 1. Cooking (Cheese) 2. Dairy substi-
tutes. 3. Vegan cooking. I. Title.
TX759.5.C48S328 2013
641.6 73—dc23
            2013007875

First Da Capo Press edition 2013

Published by Da Capo Press
A Member of the Perseus Books Group
www.dacapopress.com

Da Capo Press books are available at special discounts for bulk purchases in the U.S. by corporations, in-
stitutions, and other organizations. For more information, please contact the Special Markets Department
at the Perseus Books Group, 2300 Chestnut Street, Suite 200, Philadelphia, PA, 19103, or call (800) 810-
4145, ext. 5000, or e-mail special.markets@perseusbooks.com.

10 9 8 7 6 5 4 3 2 1

To all the animals—
so you know that you have not passed
this way unloved.

Just maybe, the moon is really made of vegan cheese . . .

CONTENTS

introduction

We have officially entered the Age of Vegan Cheese!

With two dozen easy, homemade vegan cheese recipes and variations followed by more than one hundred recipes for dishes either using those cheeses or re-creating the unique flavor and texture of cheese, *The Cheesy Vegan* gives the power of cheese back to the people. Within these pages, cheese becomes accessible to everyone, whether you are a lifelong vegan, one of my more carnivorous pals at home, or merely curious and hungry.

Since before recorded history, cheese has been one of the most beloved and sought-after foods in the world. Sliced, cubed, shredded, and spread, it has dutifully marched through the annals of time, from the walls of Egyptian tombs, where it was celebrated as a go-to ancient treat, straight into pop culture, thanks to the cheese wedge hats that have become the ultimate expression of cheesy love and standard propaganda at tailgating parties.

Although the very first cheeses were a whole lot saltier and even sour compared to what's enjoyed today, traditional, dairy-based cheese has always been the toast of cozy family dinners, party appetizers, and midnight snacks. For everyone except vegans, that is.

Smooth, creamy, *dairy* delights to the tune of Cheddar, Swiss, mozzarella, Parmesan, Brie, and so many more, have long been an epic tease, tempting and taunting those of us who follow a plant-based lifestyle. But no longer, my friends. Because now, we get to indulge, too!

The Cheesy Vegan transforms vegan cheese into the Main Street party it's meant to be, whether for a casual family meal at home, a romantic date for two, or a full-blown bash where cheese, wine, and beer each become a convenient excuse to indulge in the other.

To start, I help you get your Cheesy Vegan Pantry stocked with all the basics, many of which you probably already have on hand. Like my other cookbooks, *The Cheesy Vegan* is small-town friendly, meaning I use ingredients that my friends and neighbors in my small hometown can easily find in our grocery stores or online, just like my big city pals can in their larger supermarkets. Plus, I use basic equipment and easy techniques that are geared toward the everyday home cook, whether a beginner or pro, so you can whip up a cheesy*licious* feast anytime you want.

The Cheesy Vegan Pantry is followed by Chapter 1: The DIY Vegan Cheese Kitchen, which is full of inspired, nondairy alternatives for everyone's favorite cheeses: from a basic Cheddar (with smoked and horseradish variations), to regular and smoked mozzarella, to Swiss, Brie, and much more. This library of cheese recipes will carry you throughout the book, no matter the occasion, the craving, or how much time you have (or don't have). Also, some of the recipes go solo, relying on their own inventive combinations of everyday ingredients to magically convey that familiar cheesy flavor and texture in a dish.

Brunches, lunches, and family suppers become instantly warm and cozy when the menus include Sunrise Bruschetta with Ricotta, Powdered Sugar & Lemon Zest; Four-Alarm Grilled Cheese & Jalapeño Sandwiches; Brie & Tomato Pasta Shells; and Build Your Own Quesadilla. Or laid-back soups and salads, such as Smoky Mountain Tomato & Cheddar Soup, Swiss Meets French Onion Soup, Three Beans Steal the Scene Salad, and Picnic Pasta Salad with Sun-Dried Tomatoes & Feta Cheese. And if it's ooey-gooey, eyes-rolled-back-in-your-head comfort you're after, head straight to the buffet of mac 'n' cheese dishes in Chapter 8, and dig in!

Also, get ready to make the most of quality snack time with family and friends by serving quick bites, such as Flying Buffalo Dip, Cheddar Pub Dip, the Dynamic Jalapeño Popper Duo, and Parmesan Popcorn.

Of course, dessert is always an exclamation point to a great meal. The cheesecake chapter has—you guessed it—an array of sweet cheesecake delights: the Vanilla, Strawberry, Chocolate, Blueberry, and Banana Cheesecake Extravaganza; Pecan-Crusted Cheesecake Bars; White Chocolate Cheesecake Petit Fours; Cheesecake Party Parfaits; and Strawberry-Banana Cheesecake Smoothies.

Finally, Chapter 10 offers vegan cheese pairings with your favorite wines, beers, cocktails, and more. Whether for a swanky party or a barefoot, backyard barbecue, these buzz-worthy pairings have you covered for many endless days and nights filled with good memories, laughter, and dancing on tabletops.

My friends, it's our time to raise a slice, a scoop, or a forkful to the new Kingdom of Cheese, where our appetites for good food and fun can run wild once more!

the cheesy vegan pantry

It would be impossible to always have every ingredient on hand, but it is certainly helpful to have a pantry of basics close by whenever you're craving a cheesy snack or feast. This chapter lays out many of the standard ingredients that either are used frequently throughout the book in various recipes or have a starring role in a homemade cheese or dish that you will likely return to on a regular basis.

agar

Agar, or agar-agar, which comes in powder or flakes, is a natural vegetable gelatin additive made from various species of red algae. Often used to make such things as jelly, custards, puddings, and desserts, it is especially prized within plant-based cooking for its high gelling capabilities, and because true gelatin is made from animal products. Agar actually has higher gelling properties than traditional gelatin does, and it sets in just an hour at room temperature. Note that the same volume measurement of agar flakes is half the quantity of agar powder.

While agar is available in most natural food stores and large supermarkets, it may also be obtained online at such places as VeganEssentials.com, VeganStore.com, Amazon.com, iherb.com, EdenFoods.com, BarryFarm .com, agar-agar.org, and BulkFoods.com.

For other vegan gelatin needs, Lieber's Unflavored Jel is recommended and is available online at VeganEssentials.com.

alcohol

Every attempt has been made to confirm that the alcohol used throughout this book is either inherently vegan or produced in vegan forms by various companies. For more information on vegan brands of alcohol, please visit Barnivore.com.

The alcohol used in a few of the cheese and food recipes includes:

- Beer (dark, stout)
- Port wine
- Rum (white)
- Vermouth (white)
- Vodka
- Wine (dry red, dry white, Madeira, Marsala)

For the cheese, wine, beer, and cocktail pairing chart, please refer to page 220.

beans

Beans are a vegan's best friend; well, one of them, anyway. It's always nice to have a variety of beans in the pantry. For our purposes here, the following beans are used throughout the book:

- Black beans
- Garbanzo beans (chickpeas)
- Green beans
- Kidney beans
- Hot chili beans

- Refried beans (see note)
- Yellow beans

Note: When using refried beans, be sure to check the can's label, as many brands are made with lard.

berries

The best berries are always those that are in season and fresh from a local fruit stand or farmers' market, or picked by you. The following is a list of the berries that are used in making the cheesecakes in Chapter 9 and other recipes:

- Blueberries
- Cranberries (dried)
- Strawberries

Also, various companies make berry-flavored vegan syrups that can also be drizzled on the cheesecakes, such as the Raspberry Chocolate Syrup by Santa Cruz Organic (Scojuice.com). In stores, read the label carefully to determine whether the syrup contains any non-vegan ingredients.

bread, vegan

Just as for all products, when shopping for bread, read the ingredient labels carefully to determine whether a certain brand of bread is vegan, or visit the brand's website. Sometimes, bread will contain refined sugar, milk, butter, or honey. In addition, you can also find many vegan bread recipes online. For the recipes that follow, feel free to experiment with different bread types, including making your own, while still sticking close to the recipe.

A variety of different breads are used throughout the book, including:

- Bread crumbs
- Brown
- Ciabatta
- French
- Italian
- Panko (Japanese bread crumbs)
- Pumpernickel
- Rye
- Slider buns
- Sourdough
- Whole-grain
- Whole wheat

cheese, vegan

In addition to the cheese recipes in Chapter 1, vegan cheese is starting to become more widely available in stores and online. Unfortunately, not all nondairy cheese is created the same, taste-wise. Some reliable brands of vegan cheese are listed in the Store-Bought Vegan Cheese Resource Guide on page 233.

chocolate, vegan

Vegan chocolate is available from such online sites as VeganEssentials.com and Amazon.com. In stores, read the label carefully to determine whether the chocolate contains any dairy products; ideally, it has been manufactured in a dedicated milk-free environment. Here, both regular and white chocolate are used to make the cheesecake recipes in Chapter 9.

Also, Santa Cruz Organic Chocolate Syrup, which comes in various flavors, is perfect for drizzling on cheesecakes and is even available in different flavors (Scojuice.com).

cornstarch

Extracted from the endosperm of a corn kernel, cornstarch is basically the starch of the corn grain. Here in the cheese recipes, as in other cooking, it is used as a thickening agent.

egg replacers, vegan

Today, there are many options for removing eggs from dishes and replacing them with vegan egg substitutions or replacers, which basically consist of a natural powdered combination of starches and leavening ingredients. While various vegan egg replacers are available, one go-to source is Ener-G brand's Egg Replacer (Ener-G.com), which is made using potato starch, tapioca flour, leavening (calcium lactate, calcium carbonate, tartaric acid), cellulose gum, and modified cellulose. For this particular egg replacer, the conversion is: 1 egg = 1½ teaspoons of dry Egg Replacer plus 2 tablespoons of water.

Also, see Flaxseed on this page.

extra-virgin olive oil

Extra-virgin olive oil is the most flavorful and highest quality of the olive oils and is used frequently throughout the book. Moreover, it isn't made using chemicals. Olive oils can range in price widely, but using a less expensive, moderately priced extra-virgin olive oil is fine.

For more information on all things olive oil, go to OliveOilSource.com.

Other oils used in the book include:

- Canola oil
- Coconut oil
- Peanut oil
- White truffle oil (see page 21)

flavorings

The following flavorings are used in the book and will come in handy for other cooking as well:

- Almond extract
- Vanilla extract

flaxseed

Often recognized for its nutritional properties, flaxseed is used in the book to create an alternative to the egg replacers in such recipes as Swiss & Cheddar Sunday Brunch Tarts (page 53) and Three-Cheese Screwy Fusilli (page 181). Generally, you can experiment by replacing the egg replacer in more savory recipes with a flaxseed mixture.

To use flaxseed to replace eggs, for each egg, process or blend 3 tablespoons of filtered or bottled water with 1 tablespoon of ground flaxseed until the mixture is smooth and thick. Let the mixture rest for a minute or two before adding to your recipe.

flour, instant

A few of the recipes call for Wondra or instant flour. Instant flour is a finely ground flour that instantly dissolves in water, as opposed to all-purpose flour, pastry flour, and cake flour that take longer to dissolve. Although these latter three flours can often be used interchangeably, they cannot be used in place of instant flour. One widely available, go-to brand of instant flour is General Mills's Gold Medal Wondra Flour. Instant flour is used to make such recipes as Thyme of Your Life Baked Broccoli (page 92) and Cozy Cottage Pancakes (page 54).

All-purpose flour is also used in several recipes throughout the book.

fruit

The best fruit is always that which is in season and fresh from a local fruit stand or farmers' market, or picked by you. The following is a list of the fruits that are used throughout the book:

- Avocados
- Bananas
- Coconut
- Dates (dried)
- Lemon (juice, zest; see note)
- Lime (juice, see note)
- Mangoes
- Olives (black, kalamata, Spanish)
- Pears
- Pimiento (see note)
- Raisins (black, white)

Note: Rolling lemons and limes on your counter with the palm of your hand to soften them, and/or microwaving the lemons and limes, lightly punctured, for 1 to 2 minutes, depending on your oven's wattage, will make them yield more juice. Also, thinner-skinned lemons and limes yield more juice. When using pimiento-stuffed olives, be sure to check the label, as many brands are preserved using an unidentified source of lactic acid.

graham crackers, vegan

Graham crackers are used to make the cheesecake recipes in Chapter 9. Not all graham crackers are vegan, so carefully read ingredient labels when shopping for them. Online sources for vegan graham crackers include Sweetandsara.com, VeganEssentials.com, and VeganStore.com.

herbs and spices

Herbs and spices really do make the world of cheese go around. A dash of this herb and a pinch of that spice can completely revive, refresh, and transform a cheesy dish right before your eyes. A well-stocked herb and spice rack is an ever-evolving thing, but it will come in just as handy for these recipes as for any other cooking. Herbs and spices raise the flavor profile of the actual homemade cheese itself and whatever other ingredients it's being mixed and matched with. They can also be fun to experiment with when trying to switch up a dish.

The herbs and spices used throughout the book include:

Herbs:
- Basil leaves
- Bay leaves (see note about chiffonade)
- Caraway seeds
- Coriander (also called cilantro)
- Dill
- Mint leaves
- Oregano (dried and leaves)
- Parsley leaves
- Rosemary leaves
- Sage leaves
- Tarragon
- Thyme

Spices:
- Allspice
- Chili powder
- Cinnamon
- Cloves
- Cumin
- Curry powder
- Garlic powder
- Ginger
- Nutmeg
- Onion powder

- Paprika (smoked Spanish, unsmoked)
- Pepper (black, cayenne, white)
- Red pepper flakes
- Salt (celery, kosher, sea salt)
- Turmeric

Note: A few recipes, such as Picnic Pasta Salad with Sun-Dried Tomatoes & Feta Cheese (page 86), Tomato Gratin with Cheddar Crumbs & Basil Chiffonade (page 170), and When the Moon Hits Your Eye Cheesy Pizza Pie (page 174), call for basil leaves to be cut chiffonade style. To do this, stack the basil leaves, roll them tightly from the top down, and then carefully slice the roll into thin strips.

hot sauce

Several of the recipes call for hot sauce. While Tabasco sauce is the original liquid fire, another go-to is Frank's Red Hot Cayenne Pepper Sauce (FranksRedHot.com). For a DIY hot sauce, check out the Seitan Flares hot sauce (page 138) or the following recipe on loan from *Grilling Vegan Style*:

drop it like it's hot

1 (0.7-OUNCE) PACKET GOOD SEASONS ITALIAN DRESSING (POWDER)

8 TABLESPOONS (1 STICK) VEGAN MARGARINE

2 CUPS FRANK'S RED HOT CAYENNE PEPPER SAUCE

6 TABLESPOONS BEER (OPTIONAL)

In a medium-size bowl, combine all the ingredients, mixing well.

yields ABOUT 2½ CUPS

ketchup, vegan

Most ketchup is inherently vegan, but it is important to still read the labels to make sure you are comfortable with the product you are buying. One online source for vegan ketchup is the Annie's Naturals brand of Organic Ketchup (Annies.com).

liquid smoke

If it's a smoked cheese flavor you're after, liquid smoke is an easy way to give some of the vegan cheeses, such as Cheddar (page 28) and mozzarella (page 31), and other dishes that down-home country touch. Produced through a procedure using real smoke from select wood chips, liquid smoke mimics the taste of food produced through a traditional smoking process. It comes in a variety of flavors, such as hickory, mesquite, apple, and more. In addition to adding smokiness to cheese, it is also used as a flavoring for such items as tofu, tempeh, and seitan. Liquid smoke can be strong, so be aware that a little goes a long way, and, in some cases, can even be applied with a spray bottle for greater control. While liquid smoke is easily found in stores, one online source offering a variety of vegan liquid smoke flavors is Colgin.com.

margarine, vegan

Where a recipe calls for "vegan margarine" as a substitute for traditional butter, I suggest using the Earth Balance brand of buttery spreads (EarthBalanceNatural.com) or another nondairy, trans-fat-free, nonhydrogenated vegan margarine of choice.

The vegan Muenster cheese recipe on page 44 calls for cashew butter, which is as simple and delicious as it sounds. While cashew butter is now widely available in stores and online, here are two DIY versions:

homemade vegan cashew butter

2 CUPS UNSALTED ROASTED OR DRY TOASTED CASHEWS

2 TABLESPOONS VEGETABLE OR EXTRA-VIRGIN OLIVE OIL, PLUS MORE IF DESIRED

1/4 TEASPOON SALT

1 TEASPOON VEGAN SUGAR (OPTIONAL)

In a food processor or blender, combine the nuts, oil, salt, and sugar (if using). Process on high speed for 30 seconds. Scrape down the sides with a rubber spatula and process to your desired smoothness, adding more oil, 1 teaspoon at a time, if a smoother butter is desired. Adjust the seasoning to taste. Place the cashew butter in a covered container and refrigerate until ready to use. Yields 1 to 1½ cups.

One other quick alternative for making cashew butter: In a food processor, process 2 cups of roasted salted cashews until finely ground and then add 2 tablespoons of vegan margarine, blending until smooth. Add salt to taste, if desired.

yields ABOUT 2 CUPS

mayonnaise, vegan

When store-bought vegan mayonnaise is called for, Vegenaise is the recommended brand. Vegenaise is becoming more widely available in stores and can also be purchased online at FollowYourHeart.com, which is the company that originally created it.

For a DIY mayo, the following two versions can be used throughout this book:

homemade vegan mayonnaise

3/4 CUP ALL-PURPOSE FLOUR

1/2 CUP VEGAN SUGAR

1 CUP WATER

1/2 CUP CIDER VINEGAR

3/4 CUP VEGETABLE OIL

2 TABLESPOONS FRESHLY SQUEEZED LIME JUICE

1 TEASPOON GRATED LIME ZEST

2 TEASPOONS SALT

1/2 TEASPOON DRY MUSTARD, SUCH AS COLMAN'S

3/4 CUP SOFT TOFU, PRESSED AND DRAINED, IF DESIRED (SEE PAGE 18)

In a medium-size saucepan, stir together the flour, sugar, water, and vinegar. Cook over medium-low heat, stirring often, until thick.

In a standing blender, combine the vegetable oil, lime juice, zest, salt, dry mustard, and tofu, and blend well.

Add half the hot flour mixture to the blender and blend. Add the remaining flour mixture and blend again.

Use at room temperature or cool in the refrigerator. Homemade vegan mayonnaise will keep in the refrigerator for 4 to 5 days.

yields ABOUT 2 CUPS

homemade red vegan mayonnaise

3 TABLESPOONS FRESHLY SQUEEZED LEMON OR LIME JUICE

½ CUP SOY MILK

½ TEASPOON SALT

¼ TEASPOON HUNGARIAN OR SMOKED SPANISH PAPRIKA

¼ TEASPOON DRY MUSTARD, SUCH AS COLMAN'S

⅓ CUP CANOLA OIL

In a blender, combine the lemon juice, soy milk, salt, paprika, and dry mustard. Blend on low speed, then very slowly add the canola oil until the mixture thickens, 1 to 2 minutes. Transfer the mayonnaise to a sealable jar and keep refrigerated, where it will last for 3 to 4 days.

yields ¾ CUP

millet

Dating back to biblical times, millet is a popular grain used around the world that is rich in B vitamins and used to make everything from cereal and porridge to soups and bread, and now cheese. Herein, it is used to make blue cheese (page 41).

milk, vegan

Nondairy milk is widely available in grocery stores. Recipes here call for soy and rice milk. Soy, rice, and almond milks can be used interchangeably where non-dairy milk is called for throughout the book.

miso, white, yellow, or light

A traditional Japanese seasoning that is made into a paste by fermenting such ingredients as soybeans, rice, barley, and other legumes and grains, miso adds layers of saltiness and a gentle cheesy flavor to many of the homemade cheese recipes that follow. Also called bean paste, the lighter colored miso is used here to prevent an overly salty taste (darker miso can be really salty). While miso is becoming more widely available, it can also be found in natural food stores, Asian food stores, and online at such places as Amazon.com, AsianFoodGrocer.com, and Earthy.com.

mustard, vegan

Prepared mustard is one of those fine-line items that most often is vegan, but you still need to read the labels to make sure you are comfortable with all the ingredients, which could include such things as refined sugar. Also, homemade mustard can include such ingredients as mayonnaise and eggs.

Several recipes in the book call for dry mustard, in which case the Colman's brand (ColmansUSA.com) is suggested and widely available.

For vegan Dijon mustard, which is widely available in stores, one go-to online source is the Annie's Naturals brand of Organic Dijon Mustard (Annies.com).

nutritional yeast

Also called "nooch," nutritional yeast is a mustard-colored yeast that is used for its cheesy and even nutty flavor, as well as its power punch of protein and vitamins. Available in flakes or powdered form, it's especially effective in making some vegan cheeses and even in place of cheese in many dishes. Just to be clear, it's not brewer's yeast or any other kind of yeast. It's found in most health food stores and online at such

places as VeganEssentials.com, VeganStore.com, and Amazon.com. For more information on nutritional yeast and other yeasts, visit RedStarYeast.com.

nuts

Nuts help bring a wholesome earthiness to many cheeses and dishes in the book. Each recipe will specify the type of nuts (e.g., raw or toasted) needed. The nuts that are most commonly used throughout the book include:

- Almonds
- Cashews (see note that follows)
- Pecans
- Pine nuts
- Walnuts

Note: Cashews, especially, are used in many of the recipes because of their unique ability to help lend a cheesy flavor and texture to a dish when combined with various other ingredients. It is recommended that raw, unsalted cashews be used in the recipes throughout.

oats, rolled

Used herein to make mozzarella (page 31), rolled oats are nice to have on hand for any number of recipes.

pasta

Be sure to read the labels of any pasta you buy to make sure all the ingredients are vegan. The pasta used in the book includes:

- Angel hair
- Bucatini
- Elbow
- Farfalle (bow-tie)
- Fettuccine
- Fusilli (corkscrew, multicolored suggested)
- Gemelli
- Linguine
- Penne
- Rigatoni
- Shells (large)
- Spaghetti

seitan

Seitan (say-tan) is made from the gluten of wheat. Wheat flour dough is washed with water to dissolve the starch, leaving only the elastic gluten, which is high in protein. For anyone who still has a hankering for meat, seitan is particularly known for its ability to take on the texture and flavor of meat. In fact, some varieties of seitan are flavored to taste like chicken, beef, and so on. In this book, when seitan is used, it is the regular, unflavored seitan, but, by all means, feel free to experiment. Be aware that seitan sometimes tends to crumble or break into small pieces, so handle carefully.

Seitan is becoming more widely available in stores and can also be found online at such places as VeganEssentials.com.

sour cream, vegan

Nondairy sour cream, such as Tofutti Sour Supreme, is available at some supermarkets and health food stores as well as online at such sites as Tofutti.com. FollowYourHeart.com also produces a tasty sour cream alternative. While vegan sour cream is recommended in the recipes, another option is to use unsweetened nondairy yogurt; however, the yogurt will not be as rich as the vegan sour cream. Or, you can use this DIY version:

homemade vegan sour cream

5 (1-INCH) SLICES SILKEN SOFT TOFU, PRESSED AND DRAINED (SEE PAGE 18)

1 TABLESPOON CANOLA OIL

4 TEASPOONS FRESHLY SQUEEZED LEMON JUICE

2 TEASPOONS CIDER VINEGAR

1 TEASPOON VEGAN SUGAR

SALT AND FRESHLY GROUND WHITE PEPPER

In a standing blender, combine all the ingredients and blend for 5 minutes, until creamy and very smooth. Refrigerate for 1 hour or more to thicken. Keeps for about 1 week.

yields 1½ CUPS

soy sauce

Wherever soy sauce is used throughout the book, a vegan low-sodium version can be substituted, if desired. Be sure to read labels as some low-sodium brands may contain lactic acid from an unspecified source. Also, Bragg Liquid Aminos is a natural, soybean-based alternative to traditional soy sauce that is gaining momentum. Check it out at Bragg.com.

stock, vegetable

Vegan vegetable stock is widely available in stores and can easily be made at home, using recipes found online.

Vegan vegetable bouillon cubes are also used in the book and are readily available. As always, carefully read the ingredient labels.

sugar, vegan

Regular white, refined table sugar is often made using animal bone char and is avoided by vegans. Therefore, where you see "sugar" used herein, you can use vegan granulated sugars, such as the Florida Crystals brand (FloridaCrystals.com), or other vegan sugar substitutes of choice.

For powdered sugar, such as for Sunrise Bruschetta with Ricotta, Powdered Sugar & Lemon Zest (page 48), use a vegan brand, such as the Florida Crystals brand, or the following DIY version:

homemade vegan powdered sugar

1 CUP UNBLEACHED VEGAN CANE SUGAR

¼ CUP CORNSTARCH

In a processor or even a mini-processor, blend the sugar and cornstarch, in batches if necessary, for 1 minute per batch, scraping down the sides of the processor with a rubber spatula. Then blend for another 30 seconds. Store the mixture in an airtight container.

yields ABOUT 1½ CUPS

tahini

Tahini, a paste made from ground sesame seeds, is a staple in any vegan pantry. Often used in hummus dishes, here it pulls double duty in several of the homemade cheese and other recipes that follow. While becoming more widely available in stores, tahini is also available online at VeganEssentials.com and Amazon.com.

tempeh

Like tofu, and originally hailing from Indonesia, tempeh (tem-pay) is a fermented soybean cake. Its utilization of the entire soybean and its fermentation process empower this treat with a power punch of protein, vitamins, calcium, and dietary fiber. It has a firm texture and a nutty and mushroomlike, earthy flavor that make it a rock star among foodies. Tempeh comes in a wide range of varieties and flavors; the recipes in this book were tested with regular, unflavored tempeh, but you should feel free to also experiment with the other varieties and flavors.

FYI: Tempeh can be a little temperamental because it doesn't absorb flavors as swiftly as tofu or seitan does. The secret is to simmer it in vegan vegetable stock or water for 10 to 15 minutes (to soften it and make it more absorbent), then drain.

tofu, soft, silken, firm, or extra-firm

A worldwide favorite for about two thousand years running, tofu, also known as bean curd, is a soy product made from pressing soy milk curds into blocks that come in soft/silken and firm/extra-firm varieties. The beauty of tofu, high in protein, calcium, and iron, is its amazing versatility. With little taste on its own, tofu acts as a magical sponge, soaking up whatever flavors it is combined with, such as sweet or spicy seasonings to make the various types of cheese and other dishes.

PRESSING AND DRAINING TOFU

Before using tofu, it's best to press and drain it to remove excess water. This will firm up the tofu even more.

Cut the tofu block into pieces of your desired size, usually bite-size or ¾-inch slices. Cover a dish or slanted cutting board (with a catch pan at the bottom) with an absorbent dish towel or paper towels. Place a single layer of tofu pieces on the surface. Cover the tofu layer with another dish towel or paper towels. Top that layer with a heavy object, such as another plate with heavy cans on top of it, another cutting board, or a weighty skillet. Allow the tofu to drain for at least 30 minutes to an hour.

Do not press and drain any tofu that you will not be using immediately. Place the remaining tofu in a sealed container, cover with water, and refrigerate. Replace the water every day. Tofu keeps fresh for at least 3 to 4 days.

FREEZING TOFU

Some people prefer to freeze tofu for a chewier texture. Doing this also helps the tofu to better absorb seasonings. To freeze, first cut the tofu as desired and drain it as instructed, getting out as much water as possible. Leftover water will form ice pockets in the tofu, leaving holes when thawed. Then, either wrap the tofu in plastic wrap or place it in a resealable plastic bag, and store it in the freezer for up to 5 or 6 months. After only a few days, the frozen tofu will assume a chewy texture. To thaw, simply place the tofu in the refrigerator overnight.

Tofu has a tendency to take on a yellowish hue when frozen, but this is natural and nothing to worry about.

truffles, white and black

Created from the highly valued white truffle (an edible fungus), also called an earthnut, white truffle oil is fairly easy to come by nowadays in stores or online at such places as Amazon.com. Try to find real white truffle oil, not white truffle-*flavored* oil. It's fairly pricey, but a little goes a long way and it stores very well in the refrigerator for several months. White truffle oil is used in such recipes as White Truffle Rice-Stuffed Mushrooms (page 162); Three-Cheese Screwy Fusilli (page 181); Mac 'n' Cheese with Ground Cashews & Truffle Oil (page 199; black truffles are also used), and others.

vegetables

The best vegetables are always those that are in season and fresh from a local vegetable stand or farmers' market, or from your own garden. The following is a list of the vegetables that are used throughout the book:

- Artichokes
- Arugula
- Asparagus
- Beets
- Broccoli
- Carrots
- Cauliflower
- Celery
- Chives
- Corn
- Cucumbers
- Eggplant
- Frisée (curly endive)
- Garlic
- Horseradish (fresh, prepared)
- Leeks
- Lettuce (romaine)
- Mushrooms (button, cremini, portobello, shiitake, white)
- Onions (purple, red, green onions/scallions, white, yellow)
- Peas (frozen)
- Peppers (banana, chipotle, green bell, habanero (see note), hot chile, jalapeño [see note on page 156 for the Dynamic Jalapeño Popper Duo], red bell, yellow bell)
- Potatoes (frozen French fries, new, red, russet, white, Yukon Gold)
- Pumpkin (seeds, canned)
- Sauerkraut
- Shallots
- Spaghetti squash
- Spinach
- Sweet potatoes
- Tomatoes (cherry, canned/diced, grape, juice, paste, plum, sun-dried [see note])
- Water chestnuts
- Zucchini

Note: If your skin is sensitive to hot peppers, such as jalapeños and habaneros, wear rubber gloves when you chop them.

Note: There is a variance in the sun-dried tomato industry, both here and abroad. When packed in oil, saltiness fluctuates wildly. For example, when not packed in oil, in Italy, dried tomatoes tend to be salted; in California, they tend not to be. Taste yours before proceeding and salt the dish accordingly.

vinegars

Vinegars add zest to many dishes in this book and can range in flavors and uses. The most used varieties in the book include:

- Apple cider
- Balsamic
- Cider
- Red wine
- Sherry

wheat germ

A very small part of a grain of wheat, wheat germ is a good source of fiber and a concentrated source of many essential nutrients, fatty acids, and more. Herein, it is used to make Brie (page 33).

worcestershire sauce, vegan

Traditional Worcestershire sauce is made using anchovies, and therefore not vegan. Luckily, vegan Worcestershire sauce is becoming more widely available in stores. One go-to source for vegan Worcestershire sauce is the Annie's Naturals brand of Organic Worcestershire Sauce (Annies.com).

Also, here is an easy DIY version:

homemade vegan worcestershire sauce

2 CUPS CIDER VINEGAR

1/2 CUP SOY SAUCE

1/4 CUP VEGAN LIGHT BROWN SUGAR

1 TEASPOON GROUND GINGER

1 TEASPOON DRY MUSTARD, SUCH AS COLMAN'S

1 TEASPOON ONION POWDER

1 TEASPOON GARLIC POWDER

1/2 TEASPOON GROUND CINNAMON

1/2 TEASPOON FRESHLY GROUND BLACK PEPPER

In a medium-size saucepan, combine all the ingredients over medium-high heat. Bring to a boil, then lower the heat to simmer and reduce the mixture by half, about 20 minutes. Strain through a fine sieve and let cool completely before using. The sauce will keep in a tightly covered container, refrigerated, for 2 to 3 months.

yields ABOUT 1 CUP

CHAPTER 1

The DIY Vegan Cheese Kitchen

Although vegan cheeses have become much more widely available in stores and online, with a little time and effort, you can easily dazzle your family, friends, and party guests by making your own at home, and then using it in all your favorite dishes and so much more. Whether you are planning an easy supper for family night, craving a rich snack, or planning an artisanal platter for the ultimate wine, beer, and cocktail pairing party, these plant-based cheese recipes and the foods that follow have you covered 24/7, no matter the occasion.

Versatile and fun to make, the homemade cheeses, including Cheddar, Swiss, Nooch, Muenster, blue, American, wine, Jack, Brie, and cottage cheese, fly solo as well as find their way into various recipes throughout the book. Others, such as Parmesan Walnut, Parmesan Almond, and feta, are mainly here to punch up the flavor profile of a number of dishes. But, as always, I encourage you to truly make this cookbook your own.

Feel free to experiment with the recipes by trying different cheeses or variations of those cheeses to add ever new layers of flavor to the recipes in the other chapters. The potential combinations are endless, offering something new and tasty for you to enjoy every day. For example, if you like that smoky touch, try substituting the Smoked Cheddar or Smoked Mozzarella variations where those cheeses are called for, and the same goes for the horseradish variations. Likewise, if a dish calls for Cheddar cheese, try using Jack, American, Muenster, or wine cheese, or a combination of cheeses for a change.

As always, make sure to read through the recipes first. Some of the cheese basics do take some time (mostly for setting), so it's good to plan ahead if you're feeding a hungry crowd—or just your hungry self!

nooch cheese

Used alone, nutritional yeast conveys a nutty and cheesy flavor, helping to galvanize many dishes as both a main ingredient and a condiment. It's only right then that this equivalent of magic dust for the plant-based set now gets its very own cheese. Lively ingredients, such as garlic, white peppercorns, and white truffle oil, meet the earthy combination of cashews and the nutritional yeast in this master Nooch cheese recipe.

Lightly oil four half-cup ramekins, wiping off any excess oil with a paper towel.

In a food processor, pulse the cashews just until they are finely ground. Don't let them become cashew butter! Add the nutritional yeast, onion powder, garlic powder, salt, and white pepper. Pulse four or five times to blend the mixture well, but not so much as to make a paste.

In a large saucepan over medium-high heat, whisk together the soy milk, agar flakes, and canola oil. Bring the mixture just to a simmer. Immediately lower the heat to medium-low, cover the saucepan, and let the mixture simmer very slowly for 10 minutes, whisking occasionally. Then let the mixture cool for 10 minutes.

Turn on the food processor and slowly add the soy milk mixture through the processor's feed tube. Process until the mixture is very smooth, then add the miso, lemon juice, and truffle oil (if using), and pulse until blended.

Transfer the mixture to a glass container, cover tightly, and refrigerate for 4 to 5 hours. If using immediately after 5 hours, run a knife around the outer edge of the cheese, place a large plate over the container, invert the container, and tap with a wooden spoon or knife handle until the cheese tumbles onto the plate. The cheese may now be sliced or grated through the large holes of a grater. It may also be spread on crackers and melted in the microwave or under a hot broiler, but watch carefully—the cheese can liquefy very quickly and suddenly. If serving on crackers, decorate with pimiento slices, chopped jalapeños, and/or minced olives.

The cheese will keep in a tightly covered container, refrigerated, for 3 to 4 days.

yields ABOUT 4 CUPS OF CHEESE

CANOLA OIL, FOR OILING 4 RAMEKINS

1/2 CUP PLUS 2 TABLESPOONS RAW, UNSALTED CASHEWS

4 CUPS NUTRITIONAL YEAST

2 TEASPOONS ONION POWDER

1/2 TEASPOON GARLIC POWDER

1 TEASPOON KOSHER SALT

1/2 TEASPOON FRESHLY GROUND WHITE PEPPER

1 3/4 CUPS UNSWEETENED SOY MILK

1/2 CUP AGAR FLAKES

1/4 CUP CANOLA OIL

2 TABLESPOONS WHITE MISO

1 TABLESPOON FRESHLY SQUEEZED LEMON JUICE

1 TABLESPOON WHITE TRUFFLE OIL (OPTIONAL)

note: In addition to being tasty by the slice, this master cheese can be used in just about all of the dishes in this book even though it is not specifically mentioned as an option in the recipes. Plus, this recipe is pretty easy to double as needed, whether using it in appetizers or main dishes.

cheddar

CANOLA OIL, FOR OILING A LOAF PAN

5 TEASPOONS AGAR POWDER,
OR 5 TABLESPOONS AGAR FLAKES

1½ CUPS FILTERED OR BOTTLED WATER

½ CUP RAW, UNSALTED CASHEWS

⅓ CUP NUTRITIONAL YEAST

½ CUP SLICED PIMIENTOS

3 TO 4 TABLESPOONS FRESHLY SQUEEZED
LEMON JUICE, DEPENDING ON HOW
SHARP YOU WANT IT

2 TEASPOONS ONION POWDER

¼ TEASPOON GARLIC POWDER

½ TEASPOON VEGAN DIJON MUSTARD

PORT WINE (OPTIONAL)

One of the most beloved cheeses in the world since the twelfth century, when King Henry II declared it the best cheese in England, Cheddar gets its name from its birthplace, a small English village called Cheddar in Somerset. Now, we vegans are leaving our own sharp-tasting mark on history with this nondairy-, agar-, pimiento-, and mustard-infused version. Serve sliced on crackers with a cold beer or use it to make killer nachos, or kick it up a few notches with the horseradish, smoked, and extra-sharp variations.

Lightly oil a loaf pan measuring 3 by 7 or 4 by 8 inches. In a small saucepan over medium heat, whisk together the agar and water. Stir often until the mixture comes to a boil, then lower the heat to simmer. Let the mixture bubble away gently for 5 minutes, stirring often to dissolve the agar completely.

Meanwhile, into the container of a standing blender, measure the cashews, nutritional yeast, pimiento, lemon juice, onion powder, garlic powder, and mustard.

When the agar has boiled for 5 minutes, carefully and slowly pour it into the blender container. Return the lid to the blender and blend the mixture on high speed for about 1 minute. Stop the blender, scrape down the sides of the container with a rubber spatula, replace the lid, and blend on high speed again for another minute. The mixture should be very smooth and about the same orange color as standard dairy Cheddar cheese.

Pour the mixture into the prepared loaf pan, drizzle with the port wine (if using), transfer to the refrigerator, and let it chill until firm, at least 1 hour.

Serve sliced, or grate it to garnish or meld into your favorite dishes.

The cheese will keep tightly wrapped in the refrigerator for at least 1 week.

yields ABOUT 2 CUPS OF CHEESE

variations

Horseradish Cheddar: Before pouring the mixture into the loaf pan, stir in 2 tablespoons of prepared horseradish, or to taste.

Smoked Cheddar: Before pouring the mixture into the loaf pan, add ½ teaspoon of liquid smoke, or to taste.

Extra-Sharp Cheddar: Before pouring the mixture into the loaf pan, add more lemon juice and mustard, to taste.

wine cheese

1 CUP SOY MILK

3 TABLESPOONS AGAR FLAKES

1/2 CUP PINE NUTS, TOASTED IF YOU WISH

1/3 CUP CANOLA OIL

1/4 CUP FRESHLY SQUEEZED LEMON JUICE

1/4 CUP DRY WHITE WINE, SUCH AS
A DRY RIESLING

2 TABLESPOONS GRATED WHITE ONION

3 CLOVES GARLIC, PRESSED

2 TEASPOONS SALT

FRESHLY GROUND WHITE PEPPER

This Cheddar-inspired blend of ground pine nuts, agar flakes, and white wine can be accented with other ingredients, such as caraway seeds and Tabasco sauce to taste. Also, the finished cheese can be rolled in smoked Spanish paprika for a whole new flavorful touch.

Line a 2-cup ramekin or rectangular container with two layers of cheese-cloth, letting an ample amount of the cloth—2 to 3 inches—drape over all sides of the container.

In a small saucepan, whisk the soy milk and agar flakes until blended. Over medium heat, bring the mixture to a gentle simmer, then lower the heat and cook for 10 minutes, stirring often with a wooden spoon, until the agar is fully incorporated into the soy milk. Let the mixture cool.

In a standing blender, combine the pine nuts, canola oil, lemon juice, wine, onion, garlic, salt, and white pepper. Blend at medium speed for 5 minutes, until the mixture is smooth, scraping down the sides of the blender with a rubber spatula every minute or so.

Add the soy milk mixture and blend for 2 minutes longer. Transfer the mixture to the prepared ramekin and smooth the top of the mixture with the spatula. Fold the overhanging cheesecloth over the mixture and refrigerate for an hour, or until the mixture is fairly firm.

Using the overhanging cheesecloth, pull the cheese out of the container. Unwrap it, slice it into 1/4-inch slices, and plate with whole wheat crackers. It can also be grated to garnish or meld into your favorite dishes.

The cheese will keep tightly wrapped in the refrigerator for at least 4 days.

yields ABOUT 1 POUND OF CHEESE

toasted pine nuts

Pour the pine nuts into a small dry skillet preheated over medium heat. Return the pan to medium heat and, shaking very often, toast the pine nuts until they begin to color. Immediately transfer the pine nuts to a 2-cup bowl, shaking every so often to keep the nuts from steaming or browning.

mozzarella

First mentioned in a cookbook by the famous Renaissance chef Bartolomeo Scappi in 1570 and arguably the most lusted after cheese in the world (as most things of Italian origin are), this vegan version uses garlic, mustard, and tahini to transform it into something extraordinary. The smooth mozzarella, including the smoked variation, is perfect for pizzas, appetizers, and other dishes calling for it.

In a sturdy empty skillet, toast the garlic, tossing the cloves often, until lightly browned.

In the bowl of a food processor, place the water, toasted garlic cloves, lemon juice, tahini, nutritional yeast, rolled oats, cornstarch, dry mustard, onion powder, and salt. Process the ingredients until very smooth.

Using a rubber spatula, transfer the mixture to a roomy saucepan and place over medium heat. Stir the mixture constantly until it thickens.

If using the cheese to spread on pizza, you can thin the cheese by adding a little water and stirring, which will also make it nice and gooey. Or pour the cheese mixture into a suitable square or rectangular storage container and refrigerate until well chilled, at least 1 hour. Then slice the cheese and offer with crackers and chopped sun-dried tomatoes.

The cheese will keep, tightly wrapped in plastic wrap, in the refrigerator for about 4 days.

yields 1/2 TO 3/4 POUND OF CHEESE, OR ENOUGH FOR A 14-INCH PIZZA

variation

Smoked Mozzarella: Add 1/2 teaspoon of liquid smoke, or to taste, to the mixture in the food processor.

2 CLOVES GARLIC, PEELED

1 CUP WATER OR SOY MILK

2 TABLESPOONS FRESHLY SQUEEZED LEMON JUICE

2 TABLESPOONS TAHINI (SEE NOTE)

1/4 CUP NUTRITIONAL YEAST

3 TABLESPOONS LIGHTLY GROUND TOASTED ROLLED OATS

1 TABLESPOON CORNSTARCH

1/4 TEASPOON DRY MUSTARD, SUCH AS COLMAN'S

2 TEASPOONS ONION POWDER

1/2 TEASPOON KOSHER SALT

note: *Tahini is a thick paste made from ground sesame seeds. The more you use in this recipe, the cheesier the flavor will be.*

brie

Class and style ooze from the mere mention of the spirited French cheese named after its native Brie region near Paris. But here, high society flavor comes home in this easy-to-make mild and creamy vegan Brie, which is tasty on baked woven wheat crackers, as well as when served as part of an artisanal cheese platter or alongside sliced apples and/or pears with a glass of wine.

Lightly oil an 8- to 9-inch glass pie dish. Sprinkle the wheat germ over the bottom of the dish and shake to spread as evenly as possible.

Meanwhile, in a small saucepan, combine the soy milk and agar powder over medium-high heat and bring to a boil. Lower the heat and simmer, stirring frequently until the agar dissolves, about 7 minutes. Let cool.

Transfer the soy milk mixture to a standing blender or food processor and add the cashews, tofu, nutritional yeast, lemon juice, tahini, onion powder, garlic powder, salt, and coriander. Pulse and process until the mixture is very smooth, scraping down the sides of the container with a rubber spatula.

Pour the mixture into the oiled pie dish. Cool, uncovered, in the refrigerator for 90 minutes, then cover tightly with plastic wrap and chill for several hours or overnight.

When you're ready to serve, uncover the pie dish and invert it onto a large plate. Slice into wedges and serve.

The cheese will keep, tightly wrapped, in the refrigerator for 4 days.

yields ABOUT 2¹/₂ CUPS OF CHEESE

1 TABLESPOON CANOLA OIL

2 TABLESPOONS TOASTED WHEAT GERM

1¹/₂ CUPS UNSWEETENED SOY MILK

1 TABLESPOON AGAR POWDER

¹/₂ CUP ROUGHLY CHOPPED RAW, UNSALTED CASHEWS

¹/₂ CUP CRUMBLED FIRM SILKEN TOFU, PRESSED AND DRAINED (SEE PAGE 18)

3 TABLESPOONS NUTRITIONAL YEAST FLAKES

3 TABLESPOONS FRESHLY SQUEEZED LEMON JUICE

3 TABLESPOONS SMOOTH TAHINI

2 TEASPOONS ONION POWDER

¹/₂ TEASPOON GARLIC POWDER

1 TEASPOON KOSHER SALT, OR TO TASTE

2 GENEROUS PINCHES GROUND CORIANDER

swiss

1½ CUPS BOTTLED OR FILTERED WATER

⅓ CUP AGAR FLAKES

½ CUP RAW, UNSALTED CASHEWS

⅓ CUP BLANCHED ALMOND SLIVERS

1 TABLESPOON CANOLA OIL

⅓ CUP UNSWEETENED SOY MILK

⅓ CUP NUTRITIONAL YEAST FLAKES

JUICE OF 1 FRESHLY SQUEEZED LEMON

1 TABLESPOON LIGHT MISO

1 TABLESPOON VEGAN DIJON MUSTARD

1 TABLESPOON ONION POWDER

1 TEASPOON GARLIC POWDER

½ TEASPOON SALT, OR TO TASTE

CANOLA OIL, FOR OILING THE LOAF PAN

note: *This Swiss cheese mixture needs to refrigerate in a loaf pan overnight, so plan accordingly.*

Named for its country of origin, this popular style of cheese from Switzerland is more formally referred to as Emmental, after its native region and dating back to the 1300s. But around here, we keep things simple. For this nondairy Swiss cheese, the wholesome down-to-earth likes of cashews, almonds, mustard, and soy milk produce a sophisticated palate pleaser that can be served by the slice for snacks and sandwiches or shredded as a topping for salads and other dishes.

Place the water in a medium-size saucepan, scatter on the agar flakes, and simmer over low heat until the agar flakes have dissolved, 5 to 10 minutes. Let cool.

In the bowl of a food processor, place the cashews, almond slivers, and canola oil. Pulse for 3 to 4 minutes to form a smooth paste, scraping down the sides of the bowl with a rubber spatula as necessary.

Add the soy milk, yeast flakes, lemon juice, miso, mustard, onion powder, garlic powder, and salt to the processor bowl. Process for 1 minute.

After the agar flakes have dissolved and cooled, add the mixture to the processor and process for 2 minutes to blend the mixture thoroughly, scraping down the sides of the bowl as necessary.

Lightly oil a loaf pan measuring 3 by 7 or 4 by 8 inches. Pour the cheese mixture into the pan, cover with plastic wrap, and chill overnight.

Place a large plate over the loaf pan, invert the pan over the plate, and tap the pan to release the cheese mixture. Slice the cheese or shred it as desired.

The cheese will keep in a tightly covered container, refrigerated, for up to 10 days.

yields ABOUT 2 CUPS OF CHEESE

feta

Time to indulge in the Greek life! With its inspiration dating back to the Byzantine Empire and even making an appearance in Homer's *The Odyssey*, this vegan feta cheese, also known as white cheese, is made with miso, red wine vinegar, and favorite herbs. With an etymology linking it to the Italian word *fetta*, meaning "slice," the version here is quite tasty when sprinkled liberally into a tossed salad, but it also cooks nicely on pizza or in casseroles. Or try it with fruit for an unusual and light dessert.

Using your hands, crumble the tofu into large chunks in a roomy bowl.

In a separate medium-size bowl, whisk together the miso paste, vinegar, lemon juice, salt, basil, rosemary, and oregano. Pour the mixture over the tofu chunks and mix with your hands until the tofu is in pieces about the size of lima beans. Set aside for 10 minutes.

Sprinkle the nutritional yeast over the top and mix again. Serve chilled.

The cheese will keep in a tightly covered container, refrigerated, for 4 days.

yields 6 SERVINGS, OR ABOUT 2$\frac{1}{2}$ CUPS OF CHEESE

1 POUND EXTRA-FIRM TOFU, PRESSED AND DRAINED (SEE PAGE 18)

4 TEASPOONS YELLOW MISO PASTE

$\frac{1}{4}$ CUP RED WINE VINEGAR

1 TABLESPOON FRESHLY SQUEEZED LEMON JUICE

1 TEASPOON KOSHER SALT

1 TABLESPOON FRESHLY MINCED BASIL LEAVES

1 TEASPOON FRESHLY MINCED ROSEMARY LEAVES

1 TEASPOON DRIED OREGANO

2 TABLESPOONS NUTRITIONAL YEAST

cottage cheese

12 OUNCES FIRM SILKEN TOFU, PRESSED AND DRAINED (SEE PAGE 18)

³/₄ CUP VEGAN MAYONNAISE (PAGE 13, OR STORE-BOUGHT, SUCH AS VEGENAISE), PLUS MORE, IF NEEDED, FOR TEXTURE/APPEARANCE

2 CLOVES GARLIC, PRESSED

2 TEASPOONS ONION POWDER

1 TEASPOON KOSHER SALT, OR TO TASTE

1 TEASPOON NUTRITIONAL YEAST

Beloved across the generations, from ancient Greeks and Egyptians to Little Miss Muffet (who famously "sat on a tuffet, eating her curds and whey") and Richard Nixon (who infamously enjoyed it for his final meal as president). The grassroots moniker of cottage cheese dates back to 1848 when it was commonly made in cottages from leftover milk. Like its dairy doppelgänger, this vegan version can also be served with fruit or vegetables for lunch or used in main course recipes. Two light and easy serving options are to dot the plated cottage cheese with halved cherry tomatoes and sprinkle them with minced fresh basil, or serve it with pineapple slices, à la Nixon.

Using your hands, crumble the tofu into a medium-size bowl. Continue mixing with your hands until the tofu achieves the texture of large-curd cottage cheese.

Mix in the mayonnaise, garlic, onion powder, salt, and nutritional yeast, stirring until the mixture looks like cottage cheese, adding more mayonnaise if necessary. Serve chilled.

The cheese will keep in a tightly covered container, refrigerated, for 3 to 4 days.

yields 4 TO 6 SERVINGS, OR 1¹/₂ TO 2 CUPS OF CHEESE

cream cheese

The mere mention of cream cheese sends the imagination in so many delicious directions at once, from breakfast straight through to that midnight snack. With origins in 1500s England and 1600s France, cream cheese as we know it today is credited to Chester, New York, dairy farmer William A. Lawrence, who first mass-produced it in the 1870s, as well as other later American cream cheese makers. Retaining that signature texture and versatility, this twenty-first-century vegan version couldn't be easier. With or without the optional flavor variations, use it anywhere you would use traditional cream cheese. For example, I like it on a toasted onion bagel with chopped green onions and diced tomatoes.

1 CUP FIRM SILKEN TOFU, PRESSED AND DRAINED (SEE PAGE 18)

2 TABLESPOONS CANOLA OIL

3 TABLESPOONS FRESHLY SQUEEZED LEMON JUICE

1 TABLESPOON VEGAN SUGAR

1/2 TEASPOON KOSHER SALT

In a standing blender or a mini-processor, combine all the ingredients and blend until very smooth. Transfer to a glass bowl and refrigerate until well chilled, at least 1 hour.

The cheese will keep tightly wrapped in the refrigerator for 4 days.

yields ABOUT 1 1/2 CUPS OF CHEESE

variations

Garlic Cream Cheese: Blend in crushed garlic cloves to taste.

Jalapeño Cream Cheese: Stir in finely minced jalapeños to taste, with or without seeds. Remember that the heat is in the jalapeño's inner white ribs, and some of that heat naturally transfers to the seeds, so proceed according to the level of heat you want.

Farmers' Market Veggie Cream Cheese: Before blending the cheese, finely mince about 1/4 cup each of chopped carrots, celery, seeded red bell peppers, and the white and light green parts of trimmed green onions, then make the cream cheese in the same blender.

Hot Sauce Cream Cheese: Blend in 1 teaspoon of Tabasco sauce, or to taste.

Smoked Cream Cheese: Blend in 1/2 teaspoon of liquid smoke, or to taste.

parmesan

What better muse for a poet or dreamer than cheese? In his seminal 1350s work *The Decameron*, Italian author and poet Giovanni Boccaccio dreams of "a mountain, all of grated Parmesan cheese" and the dishes it could be used to create. Throughout the book, where a recipe calls for Parmesan cheese, either of the following two nutty versions can be used.

parmesan walnut

This simple vegan Parmesan cheese, or Parmigiano-Reggiano if you want to get all Italian and fancy about it, comes surprisingly close to the real deal, and some (okay, many) would say it's even better! With the original dating back to the Middle Ages when it was created in Bibbiano, a province of Reggio Emilia, walnuts and nutritional yeast have brought this cheesy topper into modern times.

In a small bowl, mix the walnuts, nutritional yeast, and salt together. In batches, if necessary, grind the mixture in a coffee grinder dedicated to ingredients other than coffee. Grind for 8 to 10 seconds per batch. Don't overgrind the mixture.

Transfer the mixture to a tightly covered container and refrigerate.

The cheese will keep in a tightly covered container, refrigerated, for about 1 week, assuming the walnuts are fairly fresh.

yields 1¼ CUPS OF CHEESE

parmesan almond

Its ancestor has been long-heralded, from the world's first celebrity chef, Bartolomeo Scappi, who declared it the best cheese on earth in the 1500s, to Mario Batali, who called it the "king of all cheese." This homemade Parmesan cheese, starring almonds and lemon zest, continues the tradition by adding a refreshing burst to your favorite pasta and pizzeria-inspired dishes as well as to sandwiches and anything else you want to punch up with a unique shot of classic flavor.

In a blender or mini-processor, combine all the ingredients. Pulse until the ingredients form crumbs the size of a half-grain of rice or baby peas.

The cheese will keep in a tightly covered container, refrigerated, for 3 to 4 days.

yields ABOUT 1¼ CUPS OF CHEESE

parmesan walnut

1 CUP COARSELY CHOPPED RAW WALNUTS

2 TABLESPOONS NUTRITIONAL YEAST FLAKES

½ TEASPOON GROUND SEA SALT, OR TO TASTE

parmesan almond

1 CUP SLIVERED ALMONDS

5 TABLESPOONS NUTRITIONAL YEAST

1 TEASPOON LEMON ZEST

SALT AND FRESHLY GROUND WHITE PEPPER

ricotta

1 POUND MEDIUM-FIRM TOFU, PRESSED AND DRAINED (SEE PAGE 18)

2 GARLIC CLOVES, PRESSED

¼ CUP EXTRA-VIRGIN OLIVE OIL

1 TEASPOON FRESHLY CHOPPED BASIL LEAVES

2 TEASPOONS FRESHLY CHOPPED OREGANO LEAVES, OR 1 TEASPOON DRIED

1 TEASPOON KOSHER SALT, OR TO TASTE

½ TEASPOON FRESHLY GROUND WHITE PEPPER

Ricotta cheese is believed to originally hail from Sicily or Rome. Ancient foodie and author Athenaeus is credited with first writing about ricotta cheese in the second and third centuries. The star of many Italian dishes from main courses to decadent desserts, this luscious nondairy version with its garlic, basil, and oregano power points can be spread on crackers, used in manicotti or stuffed shells, and so much more.

In a large bowl, mash the tofu with a fork. Add the garlic, olive oil, basil, oregano, salt, and white pepper. Mash together until the mixture has the consistency of traditional ricotta cheese. Taste for salt.

The cheese will keep in a tightly covered container, refrigerated, for 3 to 4 days.

yields 2 CUPS OF CHEESE

blue

Its various dairy counterparts have lineages starting with such dates as AD 879 and count the likes of Charlemagne and Casanova (who proclaimed it an aphrodisiac!) among their fans, making this one of the world's oldest and most storied cheeses. Here, this vegan incarnation, created with millet, cashews, onion and garlic powders, miso, cider vinegar, and two pinches of nutmeg, makes a smooth blue cheese spread, which can be thinned with soy milk to additionally make a savory salad dressing.

Rinse the millet thoroughly under cold running water, removing any dirt or small stones you may encounter. In a large saucepan, bring the millet and 5 cups of water to a boil. Lower the heat, cover, and simmer for 30 minutes, adding a little more water as necessary. Let the cooked millet cool.

Transfer the millet to a food processor and pulse until a smooth paste forms. Add the cashews and pulse for 5 seconds. Add the onion powder, garlic powder, lemon juice, tahini, and miso, and pulse for 10 seconds. Add the vinegar, nutritional yeast, dry mustard, nutmeg, parsley, and chives, and pulse until you reach your desired consistency, at least 20 seconds. Taste for seasoning.

The cheese will keep in a tightly covered container, refrigerated, for 3 days.

yields ABOUT 3 CUPS OF CHEESE

2 CUPS MILLET

½ CUP CHOPPED RAW, UNSALTED CASHEWS, OR DESIRED CONSISTENCY (SEE NOTE)

2 TABLESPOONS ONION POWDER

½ TEASPOON GARLIC POWDER

JUICE OF 1 LARGE LEMON

¼ CUP TAHINI

3 TABLESPOONS WHITE MISO

1 TABLESPOON CIDER VINEGAR

⅔ CUP NUTRITIONAL YEAST

1 TEASPOON DRY MUSTARD, SUCH AS COLMAN'S

2 PINCHES GROUND NUTMEG

¼ CUP CHOPPED FRESH PARSLEY LEAVES

2 TEASPOONS CHOPPED FRESH CHIVES

note: *Although more of a spread, this recipe can be made more crumbly by not overprocessing the cashews.*

jack

1 TABLESPOON CANOLA OIL

1½ CUPS FILTERED OR BOTTLED STILL WATER

5 TABLESPOONS AGAR FLAKES

1½ CUPS FIRM SILKEN TOFU, PRESSED AND DRAINED (SEE PAGE 18)

½ CUP CHOPPED RAW, UNSALTED CASHEWS

¼ CUP NUTRITIONAL YEAST FLAKES

JUICE OF 1 LARGE LEMON

2 TABLESPOONS TAHINI

2 TEASPOONS ONION POWDER

1 TEASPOON KOSHER SALT

1 TEASPOON DRY MUSTARD, SUCH AS COLMAN'S

¼ TEASPOON GARLIC POWDER

¼ TEASPOON GROUND CORIANDER

notes: *You can vary the flavor of this mild pale cheese by adding your favorite fresh or dried herbs, pressed garlic, minced hot chiles, or even chopped vegan green pimiento-stuffed olives.*

This Jack cheese mixture needs to refrigerate overnight, so plan accordingly.

Originally produced in the nineteenth century by Franciscan friars in Monterey, California, this vegan version's ancestor has long been a scrumptious pride and joy among native US cheeses. While many legends exist as to its origins and to how it got its name (one version credits businessman David Jacks, who helped commercialize it), Monterey Jack has now been transformed for a new generation of cheeseheads with a blend of agar flakes, cashews, lemon juice, tahini, onion and garlic powders, and coriander. This new take on an American classic is named after my dad, Jack.

Rub the canola oil around in a 3-cup container with a tight cover. In a medium-size saucepan, combine the water and agar flakes, and bring to a boil. Lower the heat and simmer until dissolved, stirring frequently, about 8 minutes. Let cool.

Transfer to a blender and add the tofu, cashews, nutritional yeast, lemon juice, tahini, onion powder, salt, dry mustard, garlic powder, and ground coriander. Blend until completely smooth. Pour into the oiled container and refrigerate, uncovered, for 90 minutes. Cover the container and chill overnight.

To serve, invert the container onto a large plate and slice. Leftovers will keep, covered and refrigerated, for about a week.

yields 3 CUPS OF CHEESE

muenster

1 TABLESPOON CANOLA OIL

2 TABLESPOONS UNSMOKED PAPRIKA

1½ CUPS FILTERED OR BOTTLED STILL WATER

1 TEASPOON AGAR POWDER

7 TABLESPOONS VEGAN CASHEW BUTTER (SEE NOTE)

¼ CUP NUTRITIONAL YEAST FLAKES

JUICE OF 1 LARGE LEMON

2 TABLESPOONS TAHINI

2 TEASPOONS ONION POWDER

1 TEASPOON KOSHER SALT

1 TEASPOON DRY MUSTARD, SUCH AS COLMAN'S

¼ TEASPOON GARLIC POWDER

¼ TEASPOON GROUND CORIANDER

1 TABLESPOON CARAWAY SEEDS

notes: *Vegan cashew butter is now widely available in large supermarkets and health food stores, or see the DIY version on page 13.*

This Muenster cheese mixture needs to refrigerate overnight, so plan accordingly.

As mild, smooth, and soft as the native US cheese it's inspired by, this nondairy Muenster cheese, made with paprika, cashew butter, tahini, coriander, and more, marks the birth of a new standard on the cheese circuit. It will satisfy your cravings for toasted cheese sandwiches, quesadillas, veggie cheeseburgers, mac 'n' cheese, and anytime snacks by the slice.

Rub the canola oil around in a 3-cup container with a tight cover. Sprinkle the paprika over the sides and bottom of the container until lightly coated.

In a small saucepan, combine the water and agar, and bring to a boil. Let cool, then transfer to a standing blender and add the cashew butter, nutritional yeast, lemon juice, tahini, onion powder, salt, dry mustard, garlic powder, and coriander. Process until very smooth, then sprinkle with the caraway seeds.

Pour the mixture into the oiled container and refrigerate, uncovered, for 90 minutes. Cover the container and chill overnight.

To serve, invert the container over a large plate. Slice the cheese and serve.

Leftovers will keep, refrigerated and covered, for about 1 week.

yields ABOUT 3 CUPS OF CHEESE

american

Forget the common, processed, dairy versions. The *new* American cheese has arrived in a wholesome and natural version created with a blend of cashews, almonds, onion and garlic powders, lemon juice, and red bell peppers. This vegan wonder can very tastefully be served in slices over a veggie burger and topped with a thick slice of red onion, but that's only one of its many uses. It's extremely versatile, and nice and mild, so kids will love it, too! Also, fire up appetizers and dishes with the horseradish variation.

In a standing blender or food processor, pour the water over the agar. Let the mixture sit for 10 minutes, then add the cashews, almonds, nutritional yeast, salt, onion powder, garlic powder, lemon juice, and chopped bell pepper. Blend until it reaches a creamy consistency.

Lightly oil a 4-cup mold or container. Pour the mixture into the mold and let cool briefly. Cover and refrigerate overnight. Serve sliced.

The cheese will keep in a tightly covered container, refrigerated, for 4 to 5 days.

yields ABOUT 4 CUPS OF CHEESE

variation

Horseradish American: Add freshly grated or prepared horseradish to taste, starting with 2 teaspoons.

1 CUP FILTERED OR BOTTLED STILL WATER

1/3 CUP PLUS 1 TABLESPOON AGAR POWDER

1 CUP FINELY GROUND RAW, UNSALTED CASHEWS

1 CUP FINELY GROUND RAW SLIVERED ALMONDS

1/4 CUP NUTRITIONAL YEAST FLAKES

1 TEASPOON KOSHER SALT

2 TABLESPOONS ONION POWDER

1 TABLESPOON GARLIC POWDER

1/4 CUP FRESHLY SQUEEZED LEMON JUICE

1/2 LARGE RED BELL PEPPER, STEMMED, SEEDED, AND CHOPPED INTO 1/2-INCH PIECES

1 TABLESPOON CANOLA OIL

note: *This American cheese mixture needs to refrigerate overnight, so plan accordingly.*

CHAPTER 2

Breakfast & Brunch

There are a few different things to consider when planning a daily breakfast or weekend brunch menu. Is it going to be a small family gathering with little mouths to feed before everyone heads off to work and school? Are you having friends over and hope to impress them with your culinary gravitas? Or are you pulling together a drop-in buffet for fellow revelers who will be staggering in at different times with crushing hangovers or returning home from long walks of glorious shame?

Good news! No matter the circumstances, the following mix-and-match recipes, which run the gamut from sweet and tangy to earthy and wholesome, have you covered seven days a week. Everyone at the table will get their fill with such dishes as Sunrise Bruschetta with Ricotta, Powdered Sugar & Lemon Zest, the Great Pumpkin Bread with Cream Cheese, Cozy Cottage Pancakes, You Gotta Frittata!, Swiss & Cheddar Sunday Brunch Tarts, and Mushroom-Cheese Strudel.

Or you can get downright personal by letting your guests pull together their own ingredients for the DIY Cheesy Scramble, where their choice of Cheddar, Jack, American, and wine cheese lays the foundation for such extras as chopped bell peppers, onions, jalapeños, spinach, mushrooms, and more.

sunrise bruschetta with ricotta, powdered sugar & lemon zest

1 MEDIUM-SIZE LOAF CRUSTY VEGAN ITALIAN BREAD, CUT INTO ¾-INCH SLICES ON THE DIAGONAL (HALVE THE SLICES IF THEY SEEM TOO LARGE)

GOOD EXTRA-VIRGIN OLIVE OIL

2 LARGE CLOVES GARLIC, PEELED AND SLICED IN HALF

2 CUPS VEGAN RICOTTA CHEESE (PAGE 40, OR STORE-BOUGHT)

SEA SALT OR KOSHER SALT

¼ CUP VEGAN POWDERED SUGAR (PAGE 17, OR STORE-BOUGHT), OR TO TASTE

2 LEMONS, FOR ZEST

This radiant brunch bruschetta gets the cheesy treatment here, compliments of ricotta plus sweet and zesty twists of powdered sugar and lemon. Perfect for starting or ending a morning meal, this bruschetta also has "treat" written all over it when flying solo during a coffee break.

Set a grill pan over medium-high heat or turn on your broiler. Brush both sides of each slice of bread lightly with the olive oil. Put the bread on the grill pan, and cook until slightly charred on each side, about 2 minutes per side; alternatively, broil the bread slices about 3 inches from the heating element, flipping them after about 1 minute and watching them very closely. When the bread is charred to your liking, remove it and rub the toasted sides lightly on one side with the cut side of one of the garlic halves.

To the side you've rubbed with garlic, add a generous smear of the ricotta cheese (best to leave it kind of messy and rustic looking), then drizzle with more olive oil and sprinkle with salt. Dust each bruschetta slice with the powdered sugar and use a fine grater to grate a good amount of lemon zest over the top. Serve immediately. Be prepared to make another batch.

yields 8 TO 10 SERVINGS

the great pumpkin bread with cream cheese

Autumn by the loaf! This seasonal bread recipe, with the cozy flavors of nutmeg, ginger, allspice, and, of course, pumpkin, makes three loaves, so you'll have plenty to save for later. If you bake the batter in one-pound coffee cans, the round loaves will keep well in the cans with their plastic lids in place for several weeks of sensational breakfasts, brunches, desserts, or plain ol' snacking.

Preheat the oven to 350°F. In a standing mixer, combine the nutmeg, cinnamon, ginger, allspice, sugar, canola oil, egg replacer, and salt. Add the pumpkin, water, soda, and then the flour 1 cup at a time. Beat well.

Fill to about two-thirds full three greased 1-pound coffee tins or 1½-quart ungreased nonstick bread loaf pans.

Bake for 1 hour on the middle rack of the oven, on a baking sheet in case of spillovers. If you're using loaf pans, check the breads at 50 minutes and bake only until an inserted skewer comes out clean.

These round loaves keep for several weeks in the refrigerator covered with a coffee can lid. They also ship very well in cold weather.

Serve warmed, sliced, and spread with room-temperature cream cheese and an extra sprinkling of cinnamon.

yields 3 LOAVES

1 TEASPOON FRESHLY GRATED NUTMEG

1 TEASPOON GROUND CINNAMON

½ TEASPOON GROUND GINGER

½ TEASPOON GROUND ALLSPICE

2½ TO 3 CUPS VEGAN SUGAR (DEPENDING ON HOW SWEET YOU LIKE YOUR PUMPKIN BREAD)

1 CUP CANOLA OIL

⅓ CUP VEGAN EGG REPLACER

1½ TEASPOONS SALT

1 (14- TO 16-OUNCE) CAN PURE PUMPKIN (NOT "PUMPKIN PIE MIX")

⅔ CUP WATER

2 TEASPOONS BAKING SODA

3 CUPS ALL-PURPOSE FLOUR

VEGETABLE SHORTENING, FOR GREASING THE COFFEE TINS

VEGAN CREAM CHEESE (PAGE 37, OR STORE-BOUGHT), FOR SERVING

the DIY cheesy scramble

1 (12-OUNCE) CARTON SOFT SILKEN TOFU, PRESSED AND DRAINED (SEE PAGE 18)

2 TABLESPOONS EXTRA-VIRGIN OLIVE OIL

¼ TEASPOON CURRY POWDER

KOSHER SALT AND FRESHLY GROUND WHITE PEPPER

2 TABLESPOONS CHOPPED FRESH BASIL LEAVES

2 TABLESPOONS CHOPPED FRESH TARRAGON LEAVES

2 TABLESPOONS CHOPPED FRESH CHIVES

½ CUP GRATED VEGAN CHEDDAR CHEESE (PAGE 28, OR STORE-BOUGHT)

SMOKED SPANISH PAPRIKA

suggested fillings

VEGAN WINE, JACK, OR AMERICAN CHEESE (PAGE 30, 42, OR 45, RESPECTIVELY, OR STORE-BOUGHT) (OPTIONAL)

RED, YELLOW, AND/OR GREEN BELL PEPPERS, SEEDED AND CHOPPED

ONIONS, CHOPPED

JALAPEÑOS, CHOPPED

SPINACH, WHOLE BABY LEAVES OR CHOPPED

MUSHROOMS, SLICED OR CHOPPED

This is a consummate brunch dish that you can customize for any guest list. It doubles easily for a crowd and can be most fun and interactive when transformed into the DIY Cheesy Scramble. For daily breakfasts or weekend guests, arrange a lineup of the suggested fillings or any others of choice, each in separate clear glass bowls, to create Cheesy Scrambles that are truly made to order.

When the tofu has been properly pressed, heat the olive oil in a medium-size skillet over medium heat. When the oil slides easily across the pan, crumble the tofu into the pan, making the crumbles about the size of scrambled egg curds. Sprinkle with the curry powder and about ½ teaspoon of salt. Stirring frequently, cook the tofu until dry and firm—but not hard—4 to 5 minutes.

Stir in the white pepper, basil, tarragon, and chives, then stir in the Cheddar cheese. Add any other fillings of choice. Let the mixture cook until the cheese has softened and melted. Plate the mixture and serve sprinkled with the paprika.

yields 3 TO 4 SERVINGS

toast with the most cheese bread

Use the best high-density, whole-grain bread you can find for this sumptuous toast. As simple as this recipe seems, you may need to experiment a bit to find the most pleasing result. To serve this as an appetizer or as a crispy accompaniment to one of the soups or salads in Chapter 3, slice the broiled cheese bread into bite-size pieces. Or layer tomato slices, mixed greens, and mustard between two slices for an indulgent noontime sandwich.

Heat the broiler. In a medium-size bowl, mix the Cheddar cheese with the softened margarine, garlic, and pepper.

Place the bread slices on a baking sheet and broil watchfully until toasted, turning once.

Spread the Cheddar mixture on each bread slice and run under the broiler until bubbly. Serve promptly.

yields 3 TO 6 SERVINGS

2 CUPS GRATED VEGAN CHEDDAR CHEESE (PAGE 28, OR STORE-BOUGHT)

1/3 CUP VEGAN MARGARINE, AT ROOM TEMPERATURE

2 CLOVES GARLIC, PRESSED, OR MORE TO TASTE

FRESHLY GROUND BLACK OR WHITE PEPPER

6 SLICES VEGAN WHOLE-GRAIN BREAD

swiss & cheddar sunday brunch tarts

What a festive way to begin the week! Swiss cheese and Cheddar cheese get comfy with red and green bell peppers and red onion to give you a cheery slice of "Good Morning!" with every bite. Plus, any leftovers make a great lunch or snack for later.

Preheat the oven to 350°F. In a medium-size bowl, mix the cheeses and divide the mixture between the two pastry shells.

In a large bowl, combine the egg replacer, soy milk, onion, and peppers. Pour half of the mixture over the cheeses in each pastry shell. Bake the tarts for about 1 hour, or until a knife inserted near the center of each tart comes out clean. Let the tarts rest for 5 minutes before cutting them into serving wedges.

yields ABOUT 12 SERVINGS

1 CUP GRATED VEGAN SWISS CHEESE (PAGE 34, OR STORE-BOUGHT)

1 CUP GRATED VEGAN CHEDDAR CHEESE (PAGE 28, OR STORE-BOUGHT)

2 (8- TO 9-INCH) UNBAKED VEGAN PASTRY SHELLS

$1\frac{1}{2}$ CUPS VEGAN EGG REPLACER, OR $1\frac{1}{2}$ CUPS FILTERED OR BOTTLED WATER BEATEN WITH $\frac{1}{2}$ CUP GROUND FLAXSEEDS

1 CUP SOY MILK

$\frac{1}{2}$ CUP CHOPPED RED ONION

$\frac{1}{2}$ RED BELL PEPPER, SEEDED AND CHOPPED INTO $\frac{1}{4}$-INCH PIECES

$\frac{1}{2}$ GREEN BELL PEPPER, SEEDED AND CHOPPED INTO $\frac{1}{4}$-INCH PIECES

cozy cottage pancakes

1 CUP VEGAN COTTAGE CHEESE
(PAGE 36, OR STORE-BOUGHT),
PLUS MORE FOR GARNISH (OPTIONAL)

⅓ CUP WONDRA (INSTANT) FLOUR
(SEE PAGE 8)

2 TABLESPOONS CANOLA OIL, PLUS
MORE FOR OILING THE SKILLET

¼ CUP VEGAN EGG REPLACER, OR MORE
TO ACHIEVE DESIRED TEXTURE

½ CUP GRATED OR FINELY CHOPPED
VEGAN MUENSTER CHEESE (PAGE 44,
OR STORE-BOUGHT), OR TO TASTE, FOR
GARNISH (OPTIONAL)

½ CUP FINELY CHOPPED FRESH
TARRAGON OR THYME LEAVES, OR TO
TASTE, FOR GARNISH (OPTIONAL)

Savory pancakes make breakfast particularly splendid, especially with the unexpected addition of cottage cheese. To translate this dish into a unique side for lunch or supper, garnish with grated Muenster cheese and fresh herbs. You'll probably need to double this, even for two people, because these pancakes will be gone in a flash!

In a medium-size bowl, combine the cottage cheese, flour, the 2 tablespoons of canola oil, and the egg replacer. Mix with a fork until smooth.

Rub an adequate amount of oil all over the inner surface of a large skillet. Heat the skillet over medium heat, and pour about ⅓ cup of the pancake batter onto the hot skillet. Cook until bubbles form on the top surface, then flip with a thin spatula and cook until browned underneath, peeking under by lifting a corner of one of the pancakes. Serve at once, perhaps with additional cottage cheese spread on top of each pancake. Or garnish with the Muenster cheese and herbs.

yields 2 SERVINGS

you gotta frittata!

In addition to being delectable, this frittata is also quite salubrious. It brings together a who's who of fresh farmers' market veggies, such as potatoes, red bell peppers, zucchini, and tomatoes, all accented with turmeric, smoked Spanish paprika, Dijon mustard, and lots more.

Preheat the oven to 375°F. In a large skillet over medium heat, sauté the potatoes in the olive oil for 8 minutes. Add the onion, and sauté until the onion is translucent, about 5 minutes. Add the bell pepper, zucchini, and garlic, and sauté until the pepper is soft, about 5 minutes longer. Add the tomatoes and parsley, and stir for 1 minute. Remove the skillet from the heat.

Meanwhile, in a food processor or blender, combine the tofu, soy milk, cornstarch, mustard, salt, turmeric, paprika, and pepper. Blend until very smooth.

In a large bowl, combine the sautéed vegetables with the tofu mixture. Spoon the mixture into a large pie pan. Scatter the cheese of choice over the mixture and bake for 40 minutes, or until the frittata feels firm at its center. Let the frittata cool for 10 minutes before cutting and serving.

yields 4 SERVINGS

3 MEDIUM-SIZE YUKON GOLD OR RUSSET POTATOES, PEELED AND SLICED INTO $1/2$-INCH DICE

2 TABLESPOONS EXTRA-VIRGIN OLIVE OIL

1 MEDIUM-SIZE ONION, PEELED AND DICED

$1/2$ RED BELL PEPPER, SEEDED AND DICED

1 MEDIUM-SIZE ZUCCHINI, PEELED, SEEDED, AND DICED

2 CLOVES GARLIC, PRESSED

$1/2$ CUP DICED TOMATOES, DRAINED

2 TABLESPOONS MINCED FRESH PARSLEY LEAVES

1 POUND FIRM TOFU, PRESSED AND DRAINED (SEE PAGE 18)

$1/2$ CUP SOY MILK

$1/4$ CUP CORNSTARCH

2 TEASPOONS VEGAN DIJON MUSTARD

1 TEASPOON KOSHER SALT, OR TO TASTE

$1/4$ TEASPOON GROUND TURMERIC

$1/2$ TEASPOON SMOKED SPANISH PAPRIKA

FRESHLY GROUND BLACK PEPPER

$1 1/2$ CUPS SHREDDED OR CHOPPED VEGAN MOZZARELLA, SWISS, OR BRIE CHEESE (PAGE 31, 34, OR 33, RESPECTIVELY, OR STORE-BOUGHT)

mrs. cleaver's cheddar muffins

12 TABLESPOONS (1½ STICKS) VEGAN MARGARINE

2 CUPS GRATED VEGAN CHEDDAR CHEESE (PAGE 28, OR STORE-BOUGHT)

2 CUPS ALL-PURPOSE FLOUR

1 CUP VEGAN SOUR CREAM (PAGE 17, OR STORE-BOUGHT), OR VEGAN YOGURT

1 TABLESPOON BAKING POWDER

3 TABLESPOONS CHOPPED FRESH CHIVES

Served warm in a basket, these mom-approved Cheddar muffins disappear quickly, so you might consider doubling the recipe if you've got hungry loved ones at the table.

Preheat the oven to 375°F. In a large saucepan over medium heat, melt the margarine. Add the Cheddar cheese, a handful at a time, stirring. When all the cheese is in, cook for 2 minutes, stirring. Add the flour, sour cream, baking powder, and chives. The batter will be quite thick.

Spoon the batter into ungreased nonstick mini muffin tins or a regular muffin tin, filling each cup two-thirds of the way. Bake for 20 minutes, or until a tester inserted into the center of a muffin comes out clean. Invert the tins onto a cooling rack. Serve the muffins while they're still warm.

yields ABOUT 4 DOZEN MINI MUFFINS OR 12 REGULAR MUFFINS

café spinach & mushroom quiche

This café bigwig is hardly the delicate custard quiche that suddenly became all the rage in the 1970s; it's better and heartier. The tahini, tofu, and soy milk add a contemporary and cheesy flavor and texture that mixes well with the red onion, shiitakes, garlic, and seasonings.

Preheat the oven to 400°F. In a large stainless-steel skillet over medium heat, heat the canola oil. Toss in the onion and mushrooms. Cook for about 10 minutes, until the mushrooms have released their liquid. Add the spinach and garlic, and cook for 5 minutes longer. Remove the skillet from the heat and keep warm.

Mash the tofu with a fork and place it in a food processor. Add the soy milk and tahini. Puree the mixture until very smooth. Add salt and white pepper to taste, and the curry powder, onion powder, and cayenne pepper. Process again until smooth.

Add the tofu mixture to the cooked vegetables and stir well to combine. Spoon the mixture into the piecrust and bake for 40 to 50 minutes, or until the top of the pie is golden brown. Let the quiche rest for 10 minutes before slicing.

yields 4 TO 6 SERVINGS

2 TABLESPOONS CANOLA OIL

1 MEDIUM-SIZE RED ONION, MINCED

8 OUNCES SHIITAKE MUSHROOMS, STEMMED AND CHOPPED

2 CUPS CHOPPED BABY SPINACH LEAVES

3 CLOVES GARLIC, PRESSED

1 (14-OUNCE) PACKAGE FIRM TOFU, PRESSED AND DRAINED (SEE PAGE 18)

1/3 CUP SOY MILK

3 TABLESPOONS TAHINI

KOSHER SALT AND FRESHLY GROUND WHITE PEPPER

3 TEASPOONS CURRY POWDER

1 TEASPOON ONION POWDER

1/2 TEASPOON CAYENNE PEPPER, OR TO TASTE

1 VEGAN WHOLE WHEAT PIECRUST

café broccoli & parmesan quiche

2 TABLESPOONS EXTRA-VIRGIN OLIVE OIL

1 RED ONION, PEELED AND DICED

1 RED BELL PEPPER, STEMMED, SEEDED, AND DICED

1 CUP CHOPPED BROCCOLI FLORETS

1 CUP SLICED SHIITAKE MUSHROOM CAPS

6 FRESH BASIL LEAVES, CHOPPED FINELY

1 POUND FIRM TOFU, PRESSED AND DRAINED (SEE PAGE 18)

$1/2$ TEASPOON GROUND TURMERIC

SALT AND FRESHLY GROUND BLACK PEPPER

$1/2$ CUP SOY MILK

1 VEGAN WHOLE WHEAT PIECRUST (STORE-BOUGHT)

$1/3$ CUP VEGAN PARMESAN CHEESE (PAGE 39, OR STORE-BOUGHT)

The combination of tofu, soy milk, and turmeric here adds cheesy ambience to this brimming broccoli, red bell pepper, and shiitake café quiche, which is finished off nicely with a dusting of Parmesan. Perfect for breakfast, lunch, or even with a salad at dinner, you can really treat yourself to this slice of heaven at any time of the day.

Preheat the oven to 400°F. In a medium-size saucepan over medium heat, bring the olive oil to a lively simmer and sauté the onion, bell pepper, broccoli, shiitakes, and basil until the pepper is very tender, about 10 minutes, stirring often. Set aside and keep warm.

In a food processor, buzz the tofu, turmeric, salt, pepper, and soy milk until smooth. Pour the mixture over the vegetables and mix well.

Transfer the mixture into the piecrust and bake for 30 minutes, or until a metal skewer inserted into the center of the quiche comes out clean. Sprinkle with the Parmesan cheese and serve at once.

yields 4 TO 6 SERVINGS

mushroom-cheese strudel

Strudel dates back to the 1600s, but this vegan strudel is thoroughly modern and proves that three is, indeed, company with its shiitake, cremini, and portobello trio.

Preheat the oven to 400°F. Grease a large baking sheet with the melted margarine, reserving the rest of the melted margarine for brushing the phyllo. Mince the mushroom caps and press them between paper towels to dry them as much as possible.

In a large skillet over medium-high heat, sauté the mushrooms with the green onions in the 6 tablespoons of margarine and the canola oil, stirring often. The mushrooms will absorb all the liquid in the skillet. When they have released the liquid and it has evaporated, season the mushrooms with salt and pepper and sprinkle the caraway seeds over the mixture. Stir in the softened cream cheese.

Place a damp towel on a work surface. Spread one sheet of the phyllo dough on the towel, narrow end facing you. Brush with melted margarine. Repeat with second, third, and fourth sheets. Place half the mushroom mixture on the buttered phyllo sheets in a heap at the narrow end of the dough nearest you, leaving a 2-inch border at all sides. Fold in the sides, then roll up the phyllo, using the edge of the towel to get you started. Make a second strudel with the remaining phyllo sheets.

Transfer the strudels to the greased baking sheet. Brush them with melted margarine and bake for 20 minutes, or until golden brown. Let the strudels rest for 5 minutes, then cut into serving pieces with kitchen shears.

yields 8 SERVINGS

12 TABLESPOONS (1½ STICKS) MELTED VEGAN MARGARINE, PLUS 6 TABLESPOONS UNMELTED, FOR SAUTÉING

2 POUNDS MIXED MUSHROOMS, SUCH AS SHIITAKES, CREMINIS, AND PORTOBELLOS, STEMMED, CAPS WIPED CLEAN WITH MOIST PAPER TOWELS

4 GREEN ONIONS, MINCED

2 TABLESPOONS CANOLA OIL

KOSHER SALT AND FRESHLY GROUND BLACK PEPPER

½ TEASPOON CARAWAY SEEDS

2 CUPS VEGAN CREAM CHEESE (PAGE 37, OR STORE-BOUGHT), AT ROOM TEMPERATURE

8 SHEETS FROZEN VEGAN PHYLLO DOUGH, ABOUT 15 BY 22-INCHES

note: Phyllo, or filo, dough is fairly widely available in vegan forms, but it's also easy to order from a number of online sources. Read the ingredients label to be sure what you're getting is vegan. Also, make sure to keep the dough as damp as possible while you work with it.

spoonable bloody queen marys

2¼ TEASPOONS UNFLAVORED POWDERED VEGAN GELATIN, SUCH AS LIEBER'S UNFLAVORED JEL (SEE NOTE)

4 TEASPOONS AGAR POWDER (SEE NOTE)

3½ CUPS TOMATO JUICE

½ CUP VODKA

SALT AND FRESHLY GROUND BLACK PEPPER

½ TEASPOON VEGAN WORCESTERSHIRE SAUCE (PAGE 23, OR STORE-BOUGHT)

½ TEASPOON TABASCO SAUCE, OR MORE TO TASTE

5 RIBS CELERY, PEELED AND CHOPPED COARSELY

2 TABLESPOONS FRESHLY SQUEEZED LIME JUICE

¼ CUP VEGAN PARMESAN CHEESE (PAGE 39, OR STORE-BOUGHT)

2 TABLESPOONS FINELY SHREDDED FRESH BASIL

notes: *The gelatin and agar powders need to set for 6 hours or overnight, so plan accordingly.*

If you don't have a nearby source for Lieber's Unflavored Jel or agar powder (vegan gelatins), they're available online at VeganEssentials.com.

This unique, spoonable version of one of the world's most iconic thirst quenchers has "showstopper" written all over it. Served in whiskey tumblers, this brunch starter (and/or ender), boasting such flavors as tomato, vodka, pepper, Worcestershire sauce, and Tabasco sauce, will be the talk of Brunch Town.

In a small saucepan, sprinkle the gelatin and agar powders over 1 cup of the tomato juice and let stand until softened, about 5 minutes. Set the saucepan over moderate heat and stir until the juice is warm and the gelatin and agar powders have dissolved completely, about 4 minutes. Do not let the juice get too hot.

Pour the juice into a 1-quart glass measuring cup and stir in the remaining 2½ cups of tomato juice and the vodka. Season with the salt, pepper, Worcestershire sauce, and Tabasco sauce, then divide the juice mixture among eight whiskey tumblers. Place the tumblers on a tray and refrigerate until set, at least 6 hours to overnight.

In a blender, puree the celery with the lime juice. Strain the puree through a fine sieve and season with salt. Cover the celery juice and refrigerate until well chilled.

Add 2 tablespoons of the celery juice to each glass of tomato jelly. Top with heaping teaspoons of the Parmesan cheese and basil. Serve with long iced tea spoons.

yields 8 SERVINGS

CHAPTER 3

Soups & Salads

Served together or separately, or as first and second courses, these soups and salads have been created to appeal to everyone's tastes.

First up, the soups: the Fancy Schmancy Vichyssoise brings an uppity-up down to earth and Swiss Meets French Onion Soup enhances an old favorite, while Smoky Mountain Tomato & Cheddar Soup and Bucking Bronco Tomato & Horseradish Soup redefine comfort by the spoonful.

Next, the salads do their job equally well indoors or outside, offering layers of flavor for any occasion. Lunches and picnics were made for the likes of Tomato Meets Mozzarella, Falls in Love; the Parmesan Caesar with Cheesy Croutons; Spicy Green Salad with Swiss Cheese & Pears; Three Beans Steal the Scene Salad; New Potato & Ricotta Salad; Broccoli & Cauliflower Salad; and Picnic Pasta Salad with Sun-Dried Tomatoes & Feta Cheese.

fancy schmancy vichyssoise

There's really nothing fancy here, other than the name: the magic of this vichyssoise is actually in the combination of simple ingredients, such as minced onion, celery root, potatoes, ricotta cheese, and chives that meld together beautifully. Traditionally, this soup is served cold, but feel free to break the rules by heating it up as well.

In a large saucepan, melt the margarine over medium heat. Add the onion, celery root, and leek, and cook until glassy and soft. Do not brown.

Pour in the vegetable stock and add the potatoes and ricotta cheese. Bring to a very low boil, then lower the heat, and simmer slowly until the potatoes have softened, about 20 minutes.

With an immersion blender or in batches in a standing blender, puree the soup thoroughly. Stir in the vermouth (if using), salt, and white pepper. Serve sprinkled with the chives.

yields 4 SERVINGS

2 TABLESPOONS VEGAN MARGARINE

1 SMALL ONION, PEELED AND MINCED

$\frac{1}{3}$ CUP MINCED CELERY ROOT

1 LARGE LEEK, WHITE AND GREEN PARTS ONLY, SLICED INTO THIN COINS

1 QUART VEGAN VEGETABLE STOCK OR BOUILLON, CANNED OR MADE FROM A DRY MIX

1 POUND WHITE POTATOES, PEELED AND SLICED INTO 1-INCH PIECES

$\frac{3}{4}$ CUP VEGAN RICOTTA CHEESE (PAGE 40, OR STORE-BOUGHT)

$\frac{1}{4}$ CUP DRY WHITE VERMOUTH OR DRY WHITE WINE (OPTIONAL)

SALT AND FRESHLY GROUND WHITE PEPPER

CHOPPED FRESH CHIVES, FOR GARNISH

swiss meets french onion soup

A toasted baguette slice is the cherry atop this mélange. Caramelized onions, Swiss cheese, and a myriad of herbs conspire to pay tribute to one of the world's most famous soups like you've never tasted it before.

2 TABLESPOONS VEGAN MARGARINE

5 MEDIUM-SIZE RED ONIONS (ABOUT 3 POUNDS), SLICED THINLY

SALT

2 QUARTS CANNED VEGAN LOW-SODIUM VEGETABLE STOCK

¼ CUP DRY RED WINE (OPTIONAL)

2 SPRIGS FRESH PARSLEY

1 SPRIG FRESH THYME

1 BAY LEAF

1 TABLESPOON BALSAMIC VINEGAR

FRESHLY GROUND BLACK PEPPER

1 VEGAN BAGUETTE, CUT ON THE BIAS INTO ¾-INCH SLICES AND LIGHTLY TOASTED (2 SLICES PER SERVING, TOTALING 12 SLICES)

12 (⅛-INCH) SLICES VEGAN SWISS CHEESE (PAGE 34, OR STORE-BOUGHT)

note: *Tie the parsley and thyme sprigs together with kitchen twine so they can be easily retrieved when they've done their job.*

In a large soup kettle, melt the margarine over medium-high heat. Add the sliced red onions and about 1 teaspoon of salt. Stir to coat the onions thoroughly with the margarine, then cook, stirring frequently, until the onions are reduced and syrupy and the inside of the pot is coated with a deep brown crust, 30 to 35 minutes.

Stir in the vegetable stock, red wine (if using), parsley, thyme, and bay leaf (see note), and scrape the bottom of the pot with a wooden spoon to loosen any browned bits. Bring the soup to a simmer, and cook gently for about 20 minutes. Retrieve and discard the herbs. Stir in the balsamic vinegar and black pepper, and taste for salt.

Adjust an oven rack to the upper-middle position and heat the broiler. Place six serving bowls (or four larger serving bowls) on a sturdy baking sheet and ladle in 1 to 2 cups of soup. Top each bowl with two toasted baguette slices and divide the Swiss cheese equally over the bread slices in each bowl. Broil until bubbly, about 10 minutes. Let cool for 5 minutes and serve.

yields 6 SERVINGS

cheesy broccoli & potato soup

There are two secrets to successfully making this cheese and broccoli-potato soup. First, slice all the vegetables into half-inch chunks so they'll cook rapidly and at the same time. Second, try to avoid ground nutmeg, as it often tastes like sawdust! Nutmeg graters and whole nutmeg seeds (the size of small bulbs) are readily available, so seek them out.

In a large saucepan, place the onion, carrot, potatoes, broccoli, and water. Cover and bring to a boil. Lower the heat and simmer for 10 minutes.

In a standing blender, place the rice milk, nutritional yeast, miso, nutmeg, lime juice, salt, and white pepper. Puree to a fairly smooth consistency. Pour the mixture into the saucepan, return to a light boil, and serve topped with ¼ cup of the Cheddar cheese on each serving.

yields 4 SERVINGS

1 MEDIUM-SIZE WHITE ONION, CHOPPED (SEE HEADNOTE)

1 CARROT, PEELED AND CHOPPED

2 YUKON GOLD POTATOES, PEELED AND CHOPPED

1 LARGE HEAD BROCCOLI, CHOPPED INTO FLORETS AND STEMS SLICED (ABOUT 1 CUP OF SLENDER COINS)

1 CUP FILTERED OR BOTTLED WATER

1 CUP RICE OR SOY MILK

½ CUP NUTRITIONAL YEAST

¼ CUP CUBED WHITE MISO

2 TO 3 GRATES OF NUTMEG (SEE HEADNOTE)

1 TABLESPOON FRESHLY SQUEEZED LIME JUICE

SALT AND FRESHLY GROUND WHITE PEPPER

1 CUP GRATED VEGAN CHEDDAR OR SMOKED CHEDDAR CHEESE (PAGE 28, OR STORE-BOUGHT)

powwow mushroom soup

¾ POUND WHITE MUSHROOMS, TRIMMED AND CUT INTO ¼-INCH SLICES

¼ POUND FRESH SHIITAKE MUSHROOMS, TRIMMED AND CUT INTO ¼-INCH SLICES

3 SHALLOTS, PEELED, STEMMED, AND MINCED

2 CLOVES GARLIC, PRESSED

2 TABLESPOONS CANOLA OIL

1 QUART VEGAN VEGETABLE STOCK

2 TABLESPOONS ALL-PURPOSE FLOUR

2 CUPS SOY MILK

1 CUP GRATED SHARP VEGAN CHEDDAR CHEESE (PAGE 28, OR STORE-BOUGHT)

1 CUP GRATED VEGAN JACK CHEESE (PAGE 42, OR STORE-BOUGHT)

1 TABLESPOON FRESHLY SQUEEZED LEMON JUICE

SALT AND FRESHLY GROUND WHITE PEPPER

VEGAN OYSTER CRACKERS, FOR SERVING

White and shiitake mushrooms practically dance right out of this flavorful Cheddar and Jack cheese concoction that's suitable for the most important kinds of power meals: family powwows and cold afternoons with friends.

In a large pot, sauté the white and shiitake mushrooms, shallots, and garlic in the canola oil over medium-high heat for 5 minutes, or until the shallots soften, stirring often.

Pour in the vegetable stock and lower the heat. When the mixture has come to a simmer, cover the pot and simmer for 1 hour.

With a fork, combine the flour with 2 tablespoons of the soy milk until a smooth mixture has formed, adding more of the soy milk if necessary. Stir the flour mixture into the soup, then pour in the rest of the soy milk. Add the cheeses by the handful. Simmer for 30 minutes, then add the lemon juice, salt, and pepper. Taste carefully and add more salt and/or pepper if needed. Serve with a handful of oyster crackers on the side.

yields 4 TO 6 SERVINGS

chorizo-pepper-onion stew

Although vegan chorizo is readily available online (see note), this hearty pepper and onion stew can be made without it. Just add a bit more smoked paprika and a few more pressed garlic cloves. It will quickly become the hit of tailgating afternoons and Sunday suppers with the family.

Press one garlic clove into a small bowl and cover with 1 tablespoon of the sherry vinegar. Set aside until the very end.

In a large skillet, heat 1 tablespoon of the olive oil over medium-high heat. Add the chorizos and cook, turning, until browned all over, about 7 minutes. Transfer the chorizos to a plate.

In a medium-size pan, melt the margarine. Add one layer of the baguette slices to the pan and cook until golden on both sides, about 2 minutes. Transfer the baguette slices to a plate and sprinkle lightly with salt. Repeat with the remaining slices, adding more margarine if necessary.

In another medium-size pan, heat 2 more tablespoons of the olive oil. Add the paprika and let it cook for 20 seconds, then add the onions and press in the remaining two garlic cloves. Cook, stirring, until limp, about 3 minutes. Add the peppers and sauté until the onions are golden and the peppers are soft, about 7 minutes. Add the cherry tomatoes, vegetable stock, black pepper, and bay leaf to the pan and bring to a simmer. Cut the chorizos into chunks and add them to the pan, along with any drippings from the plate. Lower the heat to low, cover the pan, and let the stew simmer quietly for 25 minutes. Add the remaining tablespoon of sherry vinegar and simmer uncovered, until the stew thickens slightly, 7 to 10 minutes longer.

Remove the bay leaf and stir in the reserved garlic mixture and the cilantro. Serve the stew topped with the toasted baguette slices and the smoked Cheddar cheese.

yields 2 TO 3 SERVINGS

3 CLOVES GARLIC

2 TABLESPOONS SHERRY VINEGAR

2 TABLESPOONS EXTRA-VIRGIN OLIVE OIL, PLUS MORE, AS NEEDED, FOR FRYING

4 OR MORE SPICY VEGAN CHORIZOS (SEE NOTE), PRICKED ALL OVER WITH A TRUSSING NEEDLE

2 TABLESPOONS VEGAN MARGARINE, PLUS MORE, IF NEEDED

1 SMALL VEGAN BAGUETTE, CUT CROSSWISE INTO 1/4-INCH SLICES

KOSHER SALT

1/2 TEASPOON SMOKED SPANISH PAPRIKA

1 LARGE RED ONION, HALVED LENGTHWISE AND SLICED

1 WHITE ONION, HALVED LENGTHWISE AND SLICED

1 GREEN BELL PEPPER, STEMMED, SEEDED, AND SLICED INTO 1/2-INCH STRIPS

1 RED BELL PEPPER, STEMMED, SEEDED, AND SLICED INTO 1/2-INCH STRIPS

1 PINT GRAPE OR CHERRY TOMATOES, HALVED IF LARGE

1 CUP VEGAN VEGETABLE STOCK, OR MORE IF THE STEW SEEMS TOO THICK

FRESHLY GROUND BLACK PEPPER

1 BAY LEAF

1/2 BUNCH CILANTRO, LEAVES ONLY, CHOPPED (ABOUT 1/2 CUP)

3/4 CUP GRATED VEGAN SMOKED CHEDDAR CHEESE (PAGE 28, OR STORE-BOUGHT)

note: *Two online sources for vegan chorizo are WhiteMountainFoods.com and LightLife.com*

smoky mountain tomato & cheddar soup

Tomatoes and smoked cheese are a natural and intensely gratifying combination, on and off the mountain. Plus, the addition of chopped beets makes this down-home soup anything but ordinary.

In a very large saucepan or stockpot, place the tomatoes, beets, garlic powder, and onion powder. Pour in enough vegetable stock to cover the ingredients. Bring to a boil, lower the heat, and simmer for 20 minutes.

With an immersion blender, puree the tomato mixture, or puree the cooled mixture in batches in a standing blender. Return to medium heat, and stir in the smoked Cheddar cheese. Stir until the cheese is melted and the soup is bubbling lightly, then remove from the heat. Add the vodka (if using). Taste carefully, and season with salt and freshly ground white pepper.

Serve sprinkled liberally with the basil.

yields 6 SERVINGS

5 POUNDS TOMATOES, PEELED, CORED, AND CHOPPED ROUGHLY

2 TABLESPOONS COOKED, CHOPPED BEETS

2 TEASPOONS GARLIC POWDER

2 TEASPOONS ONION POWDER

1 QUART VEGAN VEGETABLE STOCK, OR MORE IF NEEDED

2 CUPS GRATED VEGAN SMOKED CHEDDAR CHEESE (PAGE 28, OR STORE-BOUGHT)

¼ CUP VODKA (OPTIONAL)

SALT AND FRESHLY GROUND WHITE PEPPER

2 TABLESPOONS FINELY CHOPPED FRESH BASIL

bucking bronco tomato & horseradish soup

1 (2-INCH) PIECE FRESH HORSERADISH, PEELED AND CHOPPED ROUGHLY (OPTIONAL, ESPECIALLY IF THE HORSERADISH CHEDDAR CHEESE IS USED)

1 SMALL CLOVE GARLIC, PEELED

1 CUP GRATED VEGAN HORSERADISH CHEDDAR OR WINE CHEESE (PAGE 28 OR 30, RESPECTIVELY, OR STORE-BOUGHT), OR MORE TO TASTE

4¼ POUNDS RIPE TOMATOES, PEELED, CORED, AND CHOPPED ROUGHLY

1 TO 2 TABLESPOONS GOOD-QUALITY RED WINE VINEGAR

2 SHOTS VODKA, OR MORE TO TASTE (OPTIONAL)

SEA SALT AND FRESHLY GROUND BLACK PEPPER

PARMESAN CROUTONS (PAGE 82), FOR GARNISH (OPTIONAL)

This Horseradish Cheddar cheese and tomato soup packs a WOW! with every spoonful, to put it mildly. I prefer it cold on a hot summer day, but it's also very good heated on a cold winter's night.

In a large food processor, pulse the horseradish (if using) and garlic until minced. Add the Horseradish Cheddar cheese, tomatoes, vinegar, vodka (if using), and a good pinch of salt and pepper (you may have to do this in batches), and whiz until you have a slushy mixture but not a liquid puree. Serve the soup chilled or gently heated. Garnish with Parmesan Croutons, if desired.

yields 4 TO 6 SERVINGS

new potato & ricotta salad

Lunge for this recipe the moment the first tiny red potatoes appear. And if new potatoes are at hand, so are fresh herbs. You'll probably want to double this, if you're going to the trouble. But don't crowd the potatoes in the roasting skillet or they'll steam and never achieve that roasted flavor. And be sure to serve the salad at room temperature or even slightly warmer.

Preheat the oven to 400°F. Heat a large cast-iron skillet over high heat for several minutes. Add the olive oil, and carefully stir in the potatoes. (A splatter screen would be quite useful here.) Sauté for 5 minutes, shaking the skillet often after the first 2 minutes. Pepper the potatoes to taste.

Transfer the skillet to the hot oven. Roast the potatoes for 20 minutes, or until tender, giving the skillet a couple of shakes after 10 minutes to redistribute the potatoes.

Transfer the potatoes to a large bowl. Bring to room temperature.

In a small glass measure, whisk together the white vinegar with the tarragon and let the mixture rest for 5 minutes. When the potatoes have cooled, add the celery, green onions, chives, and ricotta cheese. Toss well, then pour the vinegar mixture over the potatoes and toss again. Finally, add the mayonnaise and thyme, and toss yet again. Taste carefully. You might want to add salt. Serve as soon as possible.

yields 4 TO 6 SERVINGS

2 TABLESPOONS EXTRA-VIRGIN OLIVE OIL

1½ TO 2 POUNDS TINY NEW POTATOES, A LITTLE BIGGER THAN MARBLES (HALVED OR QUARTERED IF NOT), WASHED AND PATTED DRY

FRESHLY GROUND BLACK PEPPER

2 TABLESPOONS WHITE VINEGAR

2 TEASPOONS DRIED TARRAGON

1 STALK CELERY, DICED

3 TO 4 GREEN ONIONS, WHITE AND LIGHT GREEN PARTS ONLY, OR SHALLOTS, MINCED

1 TABLESPOON MINCED FRESH CHIVES

1 CUP (¼-INCH-CUBED) VEGAN RICOTTA OR FETA CHEESE (PAGE 40 OR 35, RESPECTIVELY, OR STORE-BOUGHT)

2 TABLESPOONS VEGAN MAYONNAISE (PAGE 13, OR STORE-BOUGHT, SUCH AS VEGENAISE)

1 TABLESPOON MINCED FRESH THYME, OR 1 TEASPOON DRIED

the parmesan caesar
with cheesy croutons

True Caesar Salad should be served at room temperature. For this classed-up makeover, try to time the making of the Parmesan Croutons so they will still be just warm when they're tossed with the rest of the salad to take any remaining chill out of the romaine.

Pass the garlic through a garlic press into a large bowl. Add the salt and pepper and mash into a paste with a fork. Whisk in the lemon juice, Worcestershire sauce, vinegar, mustard, and egg replacer. Whisk in the olive oil until well blended.

Trim the thicker ribs from the romaine leaves and discard. Cut the romaine leaves into 1½-inch pieces and place them in the bowl with the dressing. Add the Parmesan cheese, toasted pumpkin seeds, avocado, and warm Parmesan Croutons to the bowl. Toss well and taste for seasoning. Serve at once.

yields 4 AMPLE SERVINGS

3 CLOVES GARLIC

1 TEASPOON KOSHER SALT

1 TEASPOON FRESHLY GROUND BLACK PEPPER

1 TABLESPOON FRESHLY SQUEEZED LEMON JUICE

1 TEASPOON VEGAN WORCESTERSHIRE SAUCE (PAGE 23, OR STORE-BOUGHT)

1 TABLESPOON RED WINE VINEGAR, PREFERABLY WITH 6% OR HIGHER ACIDITY

2 TEASPOONS SMOOTH VEGAN DIJON MUSTARD

¼ CUP VEGAN EGG REPLACER

½ CUP EXTRA-VIRGIN OLIVE OIL

1 LARGE HEAD ROMAINE LETTUCE, AT ROOM TEMPERATURE, BRUISED OUTER LEAVES DISCARDED

1 CUP VEGAN PARMESAN CHEESE (PAGE 39, OR STORE-BOUGHT)

½ CUP TOASTED SEASONED PUMPKIN SEEDS (PEPITAS)

2 MEDIUM-SIZE RIPE AVOCADOS, PEELED, PITTED, AND CUBED AT THE LAST MINUTE

PARMESAN CROUTONS (PAGE 82)

toasted seasoned pumpkin seeds
(pepitas)

Preheat the oven to 250° F. Remove the seeds from the pumpkin(s) and pull as much of the strands and pulp away from them as you can. However, don't rinse the seeds.

In a roomy bowl, stir the seeds with peanut oil or canola oil—about a ½ cup for every 4 cups of seeds. Add a nominal amount of kosher salt. Try adding a bit of thyme, oregano, cumin, coriander, cardamom, and/or cayenne, if you like.

Line baking sheet(s) with parchment paper, available in most supermarkets. Spread the seeds in one layer on the sheets. Toast slowly for about 1 hour, checking them every 10 to 15 minutes, and stirring if they're browning unevenly.

Store the toasted seeds in tightly sealed containers lined with paper towels.

parmesan croutons

¼ CUP EXTRA-VIRGIN OLIVE OIL

3 TABLESPOONS VEGAN PARMESAN CHEESE (PAGE 39, OR STORE-BOUGHT)

2 TEASPOONS GARLIC POWDER

1 TEASPOON ONION POWDER

1 TEASPOON DRIED OREGANO

KOSHER SALT

8 SLICES DAY-OLD VEGAN BREAD, CRUSTS TRIMMED AND BREAD SLICED INTO 1-INCH CUBES

These addictive croutons are an absolute must to top most salads and soups, including the Parmesan Caesar (page 81) and Bucking Bronco Tomato & Horseradish Soup (page 78).

Preheat the oven to 300°F. In a medium-size bowl, whisk together the olive oil, Parmesan cheese, garlic powder, onion powder, oregano, and salt to taste. Add the bread cubes and toss them with the oil mixture until all the cubes are lightly coated.

Spread the coated cubes on a sheet pan or cookie sheet lined with aluminum foil or parchment paper. Bake the cubes for 15 minutes, then stir them around and bake for another 15 minutes, or until crispy and golden brown. Let the cubes cool, then use as soon as possible.

yields ABOUT 4 CUPS

tomato meets mozzarella, falls in love

Oh, if ever there was a perfect match, this close cousin to the Caprese is it! Take this opportunity to splurge a little: Use the best extra-virgin olive oil you can afford. You deserve it. Also, you can peel the tomatoes, if you wish, but I don't bother.

Slice the tomatoes into ⅓-inch slices, then cut the slices in half crosswise. Slice the mozzarella into ⅓-inch slices. On four large salad plates, alternate the tomato slices with the mozzarella slices in rows.

In a medium-size bowl, whisk together the olive oil, oregano, and chives. Season with the salt and pepper, and whisk again.

Pour the dressing over the tomatoes and mozzarella and serve at room temperature.

yields 4 SERVINGS

3 LARGE RIPE TOMATOES

¾ TO 1 POUND VEGAN MOZZARELLA OR SMOKED MOZZARELLA (PAGE 31, OR STORE-BOUGHT)

⅓ CUP GOOD EXTRA-VIRGIN OLIVE OIL

2 TEASPOONS MINCED FRESH OREGANO LEAVES, OR 1 TEASPOON DRIED

1 TABLESPOON CHOPPED FRESH CHIVES

SALT AND FRESHLY GROUND BLACK PEPPER

spicy green salad with swiss cheese & pears

1/3 CUP CANOLA OIL

1/4 CUP BALSAMIC VINEGAR

2 SHALLOTS, PEELED AND CHOPPED ROUGHLY

SALT AND FRESHLY GROUND BLACK PEPPER

3 CUPS FRISÉE THAT HAS BEEN TORN INTO BITE-SIZE PIECES

1 CUP (1/2-INCH-CUBED) VEGAN SWISS CHEESE (PAGE 34, OR STORE-BOUGHT)

2 TO 3 RIPE PEARS, PEELED, CORED, AND SLICED INTO BITE-SIZE PIECES AT THE LAST MINUTE

Frisée is a sturdy, lightly bitter green that stands up to strong dressings and nicely complements the Swiss cheese and sliced pears. If you can't find it, substitute the same amount of curly endive, escarole, or radicchio, or baby spring greens (as pictured).

In a mini-processor or blender, combine the canola oil, balsamic vinegar, shallots, salt, and pepper. Process the dressing until creamy.

In a large bowl, top the frisée with the Swiss cheese and pear slices. Pour the dressing over the frisée and toss well with your hands. Serve promptly.

yields 3 SERVINGS

picnic pasta salad with sun-dried tomatoes & feta cheese

1 CLOVE GARLIC, PEELED

1/4 CUP EXTRA-VIRGIN OLIVE OIL

1/2 CUP DRAINED OIL-PACKED SUN-DRIED TOMATOES

1/4 CUP RED WINE VINEGAR

1 TABLESPOON DRAINED AND RINSED CAPERS

1 POUND FUSILLI

1 (14-OUNCE) CAN ORGANIC DICED TOMATOES

8 OUNCES VEGAN FETA CHEESE (PAGE 35, OR STORE-BOUGHT), CUT INTO 1/2-INCH DICE

12 BASIL LEAVES, CUT CHIFFONADE STYLE (SEE PAGE 12)

1/2 CUP MINCED KALAMATA OLIVES

SALT AND FRESHLY GROUND BLACK PEPPER

This screwy fusilli salad with its flavorful punch of sun-dried tomatoes and feta cheese travels well, making it ideal for picnics, potlucks, or as a workaday lunch treat.

In a mini-processor, mince the garlic clove, then add the olive oil, sun-dried tomatoes, vinegar, and capers. Pulse until the sun-dried tomatoes are chopped coarsely. Set aside to let the flavors blend.

Meanwhile, in a large pot of boiling salted water, cook the fusilli according to the manufacturer's instructions, stirring occasionally, until just tender but still firm to the bite. Drain the pasta and transfer it to a large bowl. Add the sun-dried tomato mixture to the hot pasta and toss to coat. Let cool, stirring occasionally.

Add the diced tomatoes, feta cheese, basil, and olives, and toss well. Season to taste with the salt and pepper. Cover and chill, but serve at room temperature.

yields 6 TO 8 SERVINGS

broccoli & cauliflower salad

This garden fresh green and white salad can be served with toasted baguette slices for a summer lunch or it makes a fine opening for an autumn dinner.

In a large bowl, combine the cauliflower, broccoli, celery, onion, peas, and American cheese. Toss to mix well.

In a medium-size bowl, whisk together the mayonnaise, salt, sugar, pepper, celery salt, and onion powder.

Pour the mayonnaise mixture over the vegetables and cheese, and toss to combine. Serve cool or at room temperature.

yields 4 SERVINGS

1 LARGE HEAD CAULIFLOWER, CLEANED, TRIMMED, AND FLORETS CUT INTO BITE-SIZE PIECES

3 CUPS BITE-SIZE BROCCOLI FLORETS

½ CUP CHOPPED CELERY (ABOUT 2 STALKS)

1 MEDIUM-SIZE RED ONION, TRIMMED AND SLICED INTO ½-INCH PIECES

1 (14-OUNCE) BOX FROZEN PEAS, THAWED

1 TO 2 CUPS CUBED VEGAN AMERICAN CHEESE (PAGE 45, OR STORE-BOUGHT),

2 CUPS VEGAN MAYONNAISE (PAGE 13, OR STORE-BOUGHT, SUCH AS VEGENAISE)

1 TEASPOON SALT

1 TABLESPOON VEGAN SUGAR

1 TEASPOON FRESHLY GROUND BLACK PEPPER

½ TEASPOON CELERY SALT

½ TEASPOON ONION POWDER

three beans steal the scene salad

This salad is a virtual rave of beans and cheese! It can be made year-round, but it's really a showstopper as a summer lunch course or side.

In a large bowl, combine the beans with the green pepper and onion. When you're just about ready to serve, before adding the dressing, toss the bean mixture with the cheese cubes.

In a medium-size bowl, whisk the cider vinegar with the canola oil, sugar, salt, and white pepper. Pour the dressing over the bean mixture. Toss thoroughly, then refrigerate for at least 5 hours.

yields 8 SERVINGS

1 (14-OUNCE) CAN KIDNEY BEANS, DRAINED AND RINSED

1 (14-OUNCE) CAN CUT GREEN BEANS, DRAINED AND RINSED

1 (14-OUNCE) CAN CUT YELLOW BEANS, DRAINED AND RINSED

1 MEDIUM-SIZE GREEN BELL PEPPER, STEMMED, SEEDED, AND DICED

1 PURPLE ONION, CHOPPED INTO 1/4-INCH DICE

CHEF'S CHOICE OF ONE OR MORE OF THE FOLLOWING CHEESES (1 TO 2 CUPS EACH, CUBED): VEGAN CHEDDAR, AMERICAN, MOZZARELLA, JACK, OR MUENSTER CHEESE (PAGE 28, 45, 31, 42, OR 44, RESPECTIVELY, OR STORE-BOUGHT)

1/2 CUP CIDER VINEGAR

1/2 CUP CANOLA OIL

3 TABLESPOONS VEGAN SUGAR

1 TEASPOON SALT

1 TEASPOON FRESHLY GROUND WHITE PEPPER

CHAPTER 4

Sides

Never underestimate the power of a side dish to swing a meal. The mealtime costars that follow not only shine the spotlight on the main course with complementary flavors but they can also easily stand alone as anytime snacks, tapas, light lunches, or middle-of-the-night indulgences.

The medium of rich, wholesome flavors is, indeed, the message in such side dishes as Thyme of Your Life Baked Broccoli, where any assortment of Cheddar, Jack, American, or Muenster cheese works; Roasted Tomatoes on the Side with Wine Cheese; Balsamic Grilled Onion Rings Showered in Parmesan; and Spaghetti Squash with Browned Buttery Nutmeg Sauce (I mean, come on... Browned. Buttery. Nutmeg. Sauce. I am in love!).

Oh, and did I mention the cheesy potatoes for all selection?! If you thought such delicacies as cheese fries, cheesy-stuffed potato skins, and cheesy mashed potatoes were a distant memory, think again. Say hello to You Say POtato, I Say PoTAto Gratin, Twice-Baked Ricotta Potato Skins, County Fair Cheese Fries, Cheesy Mashed Potatoes, and Jack's Sweet Potato Casserole. You can create an entire buffet or party theme around these recipes that works for tailgating, backyard get-togethers, holiday open houses, or anytime you darn well want to get your comfort on.

Time to close mouth and chew!

thyme of your life baked broccoli

3 CUPS SOY MILK

1 TEASPOON DRIED THYME

1½ CUPS GRATED VEGAN CHEDDAR, WINE, AMERICAN, JACK, OR MUENSTER CHEESE (PAGE 28, 30, 45, 42, OR 44, RESPECTIVELY, OR STORE-BOUGHT)

2 TABLESPOONS WONDRA (INSTANT) FLOUR (SEE PAGE 8)

2 LARGE STALKS BROCCOLI

Even people who say they don't like broccoli lunge for seconds (and thirds) of this simple and mouthwatering Cheddar-thyme-broccoli side dish. In fact, some of us (who shall remain nameless) can even enjoy it as a meal all by itself.

Preheat the oven to 400°F. Place a large saucepan over medium heat. Pour in the soy milk and sprinkle the thyme over it. When the milk just starts to boil, add the Cheddar cheese, about ¼ cup at a time, stirring constantly. When all the cheese has been incorporated into the sauce, sprinkle the flour over it. Stir for 2 minutes, then turn off the heat and cover the saucepan.

Carve the florets from the broccoli stalks. Rinse them thoroughly, pat them dry with paper towels, and transfer them to a roomy casserole dish. Pour the cheese mixture over the broccoli and place the casserole in the oven. Bake for about 20 minutes, or until the broccoli is cooked to your liking.

yields 4 SERVINGS

spaghetti squash with browned buttery nutmeg sauce

Just saying the tantalizing name of this side dish, which easily can become a main course, leaves one panting for more before taking even one bite. An alternative to pasta, and especially appealing to kids, this spaghetti squash is made all the more stylized with the Browned Buttery Nutmeg Sauce.

Preheat the oven to 400°F and place a rack in the lower third of the oven. With a gigantic knife, carefully split the squash lengthwise (from stem to stern). Scrape out all the seeds, then rub the cut and scraped surfaces generously with the olive oil. Place cut side down on a parchment- or foil-lined baking sheet and bake for 45 minutes. Then turn cut side up and roast until tender, 15 to 30 minutes. Of course, the size of the squash will affect the cooking time, but spaghetti squash really doesn't tend to overcook, so you'll have some leeway.

When you're ready to serve, in a small saucepan over medium-high heat, melt the margarine and cook it until it turns brown and just begins to smoke, 3 to 4 minutes. Remove immediately from the heat and stir in the nutmeg.

With a dinner fork, scrape the flesh of the squash free of the skin and separate the "spaghetti" strands, mounding them in the squash. Serve drizzled generously with the browned margarine and the Parmesan cheese, and season to taste with salt and pepper.

yields 4 TO 6 SIDE DISH SERVINGS OR 2 AMPLE MAIN COURSE SERVINGS

1 (2½-POUND OR SO) SPAGHETTI SQUASH (SMALLER SQUASH TEND TO BE MORE FLAVORFUL)

2 TO 3 TABLESPOONS EXTRA-VIRGIN OLIVE OIL

8 TABLESPOONS (1 STICK) UNSALTED VEGAN MARGARINE

PINCH OF FRESHLY GRATED NUTMEG

½ CUP VEGAN PARMESAN CHEESE (PAGE 39, OR STORE-BOUGHT)

SALT AND FRESHLY GROUND PEPPER

roasted asparagus with swiss cheese

1½ POUNDS THICK ASPARAGUS, DRY ENDS SNAPPED OFF AND STALKS PEELED

2 TO 3 TABLESPOONS VEGAN SUGAR

3 TABLESPOONS EXTRA-VIRGIN OLIVE OIL, PLUS A BIT MORE TO FINISH

SEA SALT AND FRESHLY GROUND BLACK PEPPER

1 CUP GRATED VEGAN SWISS OR PARMESAN ALMOND CHEESE (PAGE 34 OR 39, RESPECTIVELY, OR STORE-BOUGHT)

extras

½ CUP PINE NUTS, SCATTERED OVER THE ASPARAGUS ONLY DURING THE LAST 5 MINUTES OF ROASTING

3 TO 4 PEELED, SEEDED, AND DICED PLUM TOMATOES, ADDED BEFORE OR AFTER ROASTING

FRESH MOREL (OR OTHER WILD) MUSHROOMS, TOSSED WITH A LITTLE EXTRA-VIRGIN OLIVE OIL AND SCATTERED OVER THE ASPARAGUS BEFORE ROASTING

Roasting asparagus—or pretty much anything else—concentrates the flavors, caramelizing any sugars present, which helps it complement the Swiss cheese all the more. This recipe works best with nice thick asparagus spears, which you will need to peel (easy enough, with a vegetable peeler). Time permitting, presoak as suggested in sugared water to augment the caramelization of the flavors. And, for an added touch, style the dish with toasted pine nuts and lemon slices.

In a roomy bowl, cover the asparagus with warm water and soak for 30 to 45 minutes. Drain and cover with cold water with the sugar dissolved in it. Cover loosely with plastic wrap and refrigerate for 1 to 2 hours.

Preheat the oven to 425°F. Drain the asparagus and arrange it in one layer on a foil-lined rimmed baking sheet. Drizzle with the olive oil and roll the spears to coat them. Season the asparagus lightly with sea salt and pepper.

Scatter the Swiss cheese over the asparagus. Finish with a bit more olive oil, if you wish, and roast for 10 to 15 minutes, until the cheese has melted completely. Also, see the variation and extra options.

yields 3 SERVINGS

variation

Simply roast smaller unpeeled spears in olive oil, sea salt, and fresh or dried thyme leaves. Then scatter with the Swiss cheese.

roasted tomatoes on the side with wine cheese

1 (28-OUNCE) CAN ORGANIC DICED TOMATOES, SUCH AS MUIR GLEN, WELL DRAINED

4 CLOVES GARLIC, PRESSED

3 TABLESPOONS CHOPPED FRESH CHIVES OR MINCED GREEN ONIONS (USE A MINI-PROCESSOR)

2 TABLESPOONS DRY MARSALA OR MADEIRA (OPTIONAL)

SALT AND FRESHLY GROUND BLACK PEPPER

1 CUP FRESH VEGAN BREAD CRUMBS

1½ CUPS GRATED VEGAN WINE OR CHEDDAR CHEESE (PAGE 30 OR 28, RESPECTIVELY, OR STORE-BOUGHT)

2 TABLESPOONS EXTRA-VIRGIN OLIVE OIL

This roasted side dish of diced tomatoes, garlic, chives, and wine cheese easily doubles as an enticing year-round lunch.

Preheat the oven to 350°F. In a large bowl, mix the tomatoes, garlic, 2½ tablespoons of the chives, and Marsala (if using). Season to taste with salt and pepper, and transfer to a 1½-quart gratin dish.

In a large bowl, mix the bread crumbs, wine cheese, and olive oil well. Season the mixture to taste with salt and pepper, and sprinkle it over the tomatoes.

Bake until the juices bubble and the topping is golden brown, about 40 minutes. Let the tomatoes stand for 10 minutes. Sprinkle with the remaining ½ teaspoon of chives and serve.

yields 4 SIDE DISHES OR 2 AMPLE MAIN COURSE SERVINGS

balsamic grilled onion rings showered in parmesan

There's nothing like a grill to transform onions into a charred master-piece. Also, it's time to splurge again: use the best balsamic vinegar you can afford and shower yourself with the good life in every bite!

Heat a grill to medium-low heat. While it heats, trim the stems off the onions, slice them in half crosswise, and separate them into large rings. Rub the onion rings all over with the olive oil and place them, large side down, directly onto the grill.

Grill until blackened on the bottom, turning them as needed. You will prob-ably have to do this in batches. If you need to, keep the onions warm in a preheated 250°F oven.

When ready to serve, plate the onions and shower them with shards of the Parmesan cheese. Finish with droplets of balsamic vinegar.

yields 2 TO 4 SERVINGS

3 LARGE WHITE ONIONS

3 TABLESPOONS EXTRA-VIRGIN OLIVE OIL

1 CUP VEGAN PARMESAN CHEESE SHARDS (PAGE 39, OR STORE-BOUGHT)

2 TABLESPOONS BALSAMIC VINEGAR (SEE HEADNOTE)

you say POtato, i say poTAto gratin

2 TABLESPOONS EXTRA-VIRGIN OLIVE OIL

2 POUNDS YUKON GOLD OR RUSSET POTATOES, PEELED AND SLICED $\frac{1}{16}$-INCH THICK (ABOUT 6 CUPS)

1$\frac{1}{2}$ TEASPOONS SALT

FRESHLY GROUND BLACK PEPPER

2 CUPS GRATED VEGAN SWISS CHEESE (PAGE 34, OR STORE-BOUGHT)

5 TABLESPOONS VEGAN MARGARINE

1 CUP VEGAN VEGETABLE STOCK (A BIT MORE IF YOU USE RUSSETS— THEY'RE THIRSTIER)

This oldie-but-goodie side should really just be called OMG! We're talking layer upon layer *upon layer* of Swiss cheese, potatoes, seasonings, and vegetable stock. My friends, some things are not too good to be true!

Preheat the oven to 425°F. Rub the olive oil all over the inside of a 1$\frac{1}{2}$-quart gratin dish (about 11 by 8 by 2 inches).

Overlap one-third of the potato slices in one layer in the dish. Sprinkle with $\frac{1}{2}$ teaspoon of salt, some pepper, and one-third of the Swiss cheese, then dot with margarine.

Repeat with two more layers of potatoes, Swiss cheese, margarine, and seasoning. Pour the vegetable stock over the potatoes.

Bake in the middle of the oven for 30 minutes. Lower the temperature to 350°F and carefully tilt the pan to baste the top layer of potatoes with the stock in the pan. Bake for 15 minutes longer, or until golden brown.

yields 2 AMPLE SERVINGS

parmesan garlic bread

I've never had one crumb of this cheesy garlic bread left over. Serve it alone as a kid-approved snack, perhaps with a favorite heated pizza or spaghetti sauce for dipping, or with pasta, soups, and salads.

Preheat the broiler. In a medium-size skillet over medium heat, melt the margarine. Using a garlic press, mash the garlic cloves into the melted margarine. Stir well. Brush the bread halves with the margarine mixture, using it all up. Scatter the Parmesan cheese over the bread. Sprinkle lightly with the paprika.

Broil until golden brown, being very careful to watch it closely. It only takes 90 seconds or so. Cut into inch-wide wedges and serve at once.

yields ENOUGH FOR 3 TO 4 PEOPLE

8 TABLESPOONS (1 STICK) VEGAN MARGARINE

4 CLOVES GARLIC

1 LOAF VEGAN ITALIAN OR FRENCH BREAD, HALVED LENGTHWISE

¼ CUP VEGAN PARMESAN CHEESE (PAGE 39, OR STORE-BOUGHT)

1 TO 2 TEASPOONS SMOKED SPANISH PAPRIKA

FRESHLY GROUND BLACK PEPPER

you say POtato, i say poTAto gratin

2 TABLESPOONS EXTRA-VIRGIN OLIVE OIL

2 POUNDS YUKON GOLD OR RUSSET POTATOES, PEELED AND SLICED $^1/_{16}$-INCH THICK (ABOUT 6 CUPS)

$1^1/_2$ TEASPOONS SALT

FRESHLY GROUND BLACK PEPPER

2 CUPS GRATED VEGAN SWISS CHEESE (PAGE 34, OR STORE-BOUGHT)

5 TABLESPOONS VEGAN MARGARINE

1 CUP VEGAN VEGETABLE STOCK (A BIT MORE IF YOU USE RUSSETS— THEY'RE THIRSTIER)

This oldie-but-goodie side should really just be called OMG! We're talking layer upon layer *upon layer* of Swiss cheese, potatoes, seasonings, and vegetable stock. My friends, some things are not too good to be true!

Preheat the oven to 425°F. Rub the olive oil all over the inside of a $1^1/_2$-quart gratin dish (about 11 by 8 by 2 inches).

Overlap one-third of the potato slices in one layer in the dish. Sprinkle with $^1/_2$ teaspoon of salt, some pepper, and one-third of the Swiss cheese, then dot with margarine.

Repeat with two more layers of potatoes, Swiss cheese, margarine, and seasoning. Pour the vegetable stock over the potatoes.

Bake in the middle of the oven for 30 minutes. Lower the temperature to 350°F and carefully tilt the pan to baste the top layer of potatoes with the stock in the pan. Bake for 15 minutes longer, or until golden brown.

yields 2 AMPLE SERVINGS

twice-baked ricotta potato skins

An irresistible indulgence, these ricotta potatoes really belong as part of a romantic dinner for two, yet they'll also be a welcome sight for a table full of hungry eyes. Then again, "midnight snack for one" has a certain ring to it as well!

Preheat the oven to 425°F. Rub the potatoes with a bit of salt and pierce twice with a fork (don't worry if some salt falls off). Place the potatoes on a baking sheet and bake until the skin is nice and crispy and the insides are tender when pierced with a fork, 60 to 70 minutes.

When the potatoes have cooled enough to handle, slice off the tops lengthwise with a sharp knife. Scoop out the insides, leaving about ¼ inch of flesh around skin; transfer the potato flesh to a bowl. Add the ricotta cheese, margarine, chives, and remaining salt and pepper; mash with a fork or potato masher until combined.

Stuff the potato skins with the potato mixture. Return the potatoes to the oven and bake until heated through, about 10 minutes. Run under the broiler for another 1 to 2 minutes, until the tops are golden brown and crisp. Serve hot, topped with additional ricotta cheese, if desired.

yields 2 AMPLE SERVINGS

2 (10- TO 12-OUNCE) LARGE RUSSET POTATOES, SCRUBBED WELL

1 TEASPOON KOSHER SALT

¼ CUP VEGAN RICOTTA CHEESE (PAGE 40, OR STORE-BOUGHT), PLUS MORE FOR SERVING

1 TABLESPOON VEGAN MARGARINE, AT ROOM TEMPERATURE

2 TEASPOONS CHOPPED FRESH CHIVES

A FEW GRINDS OF BLACK PEPPER

county fair cheese fries

1 (28-OUNCE) PACKAGE FROZEN
FRENCH FRIES

SALT AND FRESHLY GROUND BLACK
PEPPER

1 CUP SHREDDED VEGAN CHEDDAR
CHEESE (PAGE 28, OR STORE-BOUGHT)

2 TO 3 JALAPEÑOS, STEMMED AND
THINLY SLICED (OPTIONAL)

VEGAN KETCHUP, FOR SERVING

There's a fair in the air! Deep-frying your own potatoes gives undeniably delish results, but this quick and easy recipe works very well with frozen purchased fries, which bake up beautifully for last-minute meals and snacks.

Preheat the oven to 400°F. Line a baking sheet with parchment paper or aluminum foil. Spread the frozen fries in a single layer on the baking sheet.

Bake in the hot oven for 15 minutes. Sprinkle the fries generously with the salt and pepper, then scatter the Cheddar cheese evenly over the fries. Return them to the oven for 5 to 10 minutes, or until the cheese has melted. Scatter the fries and cheese with the jalapeños (if using) and serve promptly with ramekins of ketchup.

yields 3 TO 4 SERVINGS

cheesy mashed potatoes

I know! Right?! Cheesy . . . Mashed . . . Potatoes! This is one side dish that goes with absolutely everything.

In a roomy saucepan in cold water to cover, place the potato squares. Bring to a boil over medium-high heat. Lower the heat to medium and let the potatoes bubble away for 20 minutes, or until very tender but not mushy. Drain the potatoes and pass them through a ricer (or mash with a potato masher). Stir in the margarine, soy milk, and cream cheese, taste carefully, and season with salt and white pepper.

yields 4 SERVINGS

2 POUNDS YUKON GOLD POTATOES, PEELED AND SLICED INTO 1-INCH SQUARES

6 TO 8 TABLESPOONS VEGAN MARGARINE

$1/2$ CUP SOY MILK

$1/2$ TO $3/4$ CUP VEGAN CREAM CHEESE, AT ROOM TEMPERATURE (PAGE 37, OR STORE-BOUGHT)

SALT AND FRESHLY GROUND WHITE PEPPER

note: *If you don't have a ricer—which resembles a giant garlic press—get one, because it's useful in so many vegan recipes, from perfect fluffy mashed potatoes to gnocchi to mashed roasted vegetables. If you can splurge on a stainless-steel ricer, it will last for generations.*

jack's sweet potato casserole

3 MEDIUM-LARGE SWEET POTATOES, PEELED AND SLICED INTO 1-INCH CUBES

3 TABLESPOONS VEGAN SOUR CREAM (PAGE 17, OR STORE-BOUGHT)

1 TEASPOON MINCED FRESH ROSEMARY LEAVES

1 TEASPOON MINCED FRESH THYME LEAVES

1 CUP SHREDDED VEGAN JACK CHEESE (PAGE 42, OR STORE-BOUGHT)

A distant relative of the potato, here sweet potatoes join rosemary, thyme, and shredded Jack cheese to create a fantastic holiday head turner that can also easily be served anytime as a weeknight side dish.

In a medium-size saucepan with enough water to cover, cook the potato cubes for 15 to 20 minutes after the water comes to a boil. Drain the potatoes, and when they're just cool enough to handle, press them into a large bowl using a ricer (see note on page 107) or mash them in the bowl with a potato masher.

Preheat the oven to 350°F. Add the sour cream to the potato bowl and blend well with a fork. Add the rosemary, thyme, and half the Jack cheese, and stir well.

Transfer the mixture to a gratin or casserole dish. Scatter the remaining cheese over the top and bake for 15 minutes, or until the cheese has melted and the potatoes are bubbling. Serve warm.

yields 4 TO 6 SERVINGS

CHAPTER 5

Sandwiches

To get you over that midday hump, whether at home or at work, the following sandwich recipes will do the job.

If it's an old standby with a new twist you're pining for, look no further than the Grilled Cheese Trio: Grilled Cheese & Tomato, the King's Grilled Cheese & Peanut Butter, and Four-Alarm Grilled Cheese & Jalapeño draw from tradition, rock and roll, and one of the hottest veggies on the planet to go above and beyond the call of lunch duty. I guarantee you that these are not your momma's grilled cheese sandwiches!

If it's a different kind of noontime sandwich you're craving, your lunch bucket will never be the same after boasting the likes of Avocado & Parmesan Pita Lunch Rush; Outta the Park Shiitake Sliders with your choice of Cheddar, American, Jack, Muenster, or wine cheese topper; Black Bean & Jalapeño Tacos; Lulu's Finger Sandwiches (plus julep); Smoked Seitan & Avocado Panini; the Super Hero; the Mile-High Club; and Reuben, the Magnificent.

And, when you want to convey an authentic sense of *mi casa es su casa* with every bite, head straight for Build Your Own Quesadilla. Here, Jack and Cheddar cheese meld with eater's choice of sliced pimiento-stuffed green olives, jalapeños, sautéed mushrooms and onions, tomatoes, red bell peppers, and more.

the grilled cheese trio

Time for gourmet to meet greasy spoon, when you serve up these super-amped grilled cheese sandwiches. Because they are so simple and manageable, you can offer family and friends, from fussy six-year-olds to Velveeta devotees, their choice for a mind-blowing easy meal anytime. Also, consider rounding out lunch hour by accompanying these with a soup or salad from Chapter 3. Or call upon your inner culinary artist and play around with grilled cheese combos, such as Brie and pear, Cheddar and apple, and cream cheese and cinnamon.

four-alarm grilled cheese & jalapeño sandwiches

Some like it hot, *really hot*! When you get a load of these four-alarm sandwiches filled with Jack or Muenster cheese, plum tomatoes, shallots, and jalapeños, the love will be scorching.

Heat a large skillet over low heat.

Spread the margarine onto one side of two slices of the bread. Place both pieces, buttered sides down, in the warm skillet. Place two slices of the Jack cheese on each slice of bread in the skillet and top with slices of tomatoes, then scatter with the minced shallots and jalapeño slices. Butter one side of the remaining two slices of bread and place one over each sandwich in the skillet, buttered side up. When the bottoms of the sandwiches are well toasted, flip them over with a spatula and brown on the other side. Serve hot.

yields 2 SANDWICHES

(CONTINUES)

four-alarm grilled cheese & jalapeño sandwiches

4 TABLESPOONS VEGAN MARGARINE, AT ROOM TEMPERATURE

4 SLICES VEGAN SOURDOUGH BREAD

4 SLICES VEGAN JACK OR MUENSTER CHEESE (PAGE 42 OR 44, RESPECTIVELY, OR STORE-BOUGHT)

2 PLUM TOMATOES, STEMMED AND SLICED THINLY

2 SHALLOTS, PEELED AND MINCED

2 MEDIUM-SIZE JALAPEÑOS, STEMMED AND SLICED THINLY (SEE NOTE)

note: *To select your desired heat level, know that the more white flecks that appear on the outer skin of a jalapeño, the hotter it is likely to be. But the only way to know for sure is to taste one—carefully! Most of the heat is contained in the white inner ribs and the seeds closest to them.*

grilled cheese & tomato sandwiches

3 TABLESPOONS VEGAN MARGARINE

4 SLICES VEGAN SOFT WHOLE WHEAT BREAD

4 SLICES VEGAN CHEDDAR, JACK, MUENSTER, OR AMERICAN CHEESE (PAGES 28, 42, 44, OR 45, RESPECTIVELY, OR STORE-BOUGHT)

1 LARGE RIPE TOMATO, STEMMED, PEELED, AND SLICED ¼- TO ½-INCH THICK

grilled cheese & tomato sandwiches

This is ultimate gratification between two slices of bread. Be careful not to serve these while they're too hot, though, as the tomatoes can really retain a lot of heat. I like to accompany mine with one or two large, thick dill pickles on the side.

Heat a nonstick skillet over medium heat. Slather one side of all four bread slices with the margarine.

For each sandwich: Place one slice, buttered side down, in the skillet. Put two cheese slices onto the bread, then one to two tomato slices, and place a second bread slice, buttered side up, over all.

Cook the sandwiches until nicely browned, then carefully flip them over and cook for 2 to 3 minutes longer. Serve warm.

yields 2 SANDWICHES

the king's grilled cheese & peanut butter sandwiches

Yep, you read it correctly: grilled cheese *and* peanut butter! Elvis would have gone gaga over these, though he probably would have added some sliced bananas. The sweet nuttiness of the peanut butter pairs nicely with the sharp twang of the Cheddar cheese to deliver a warm sandwich that is, indeed, worth a king's ransom.

Heat a large skillet over medium heat.

For each sandwich: Spread one slice of the bread with peanut butter, and place two slices of Cheddar cheese over the peanut butter. Top with a second slice of bread. Spread the margarine on both outer sides of the sandwich.

Place both sandwiches in the heated skillet. Fry the sandwiches on both sides until golden brown, about 4 minutes. Serve hot.

yields 2 SANDWICHES

---

the king's grilled cheese & peanut butter sandwiches

4 SLICES VEGAN SOFT WHOLE WHEAT BREAD

4 TABLESPOONS SMOOTH OR CHUNKY VEGAN PEANUT BUTTER (SEE NOTE)

4 SLICES VEGAN CHEDDAR CHEESE (PAGE 28, OR STORE-BOUGHT)

3 TO 4 TABLESPOONS VEGAN MARGARINE, AT ROOM TEMPERATURE

note: *Some peanut butters contain ingredients that are not vegan, so be sure to read labels and ingredient lists when making your choice.*

reuben, the magnificent

2 CUPS VEGAN VEGETABLE STOCK

2 CLOVES GARLIC, PRESSED

2 TABLESPOONS VEGAN LOW-SODIUM
SOY SAUCE

2 SHALLOTS, PEELED AND MINCED

½ POUND TEMPEH, CARVED INTO
FOUR EQUAL SQUARES

8 SLICES VEGAN PUMPERNICKEL
OR RYE BREAD

½ CUP VEGAN THOUSAND ISLAND
DRESSING (SEE NOTE)

1 CUP SAUERKRAUT, DRAINED

1 CUP SHREDDED VEGAN SWISS CHEESE
(PAGE 34, OR STORE-BOUGHT)

note: *Many bottled Thousand Island dressings are vegan, but check the label before buying. As you know, non-vegan ingredients can pop up in some very unlikely places.*

While the origins of the original Reuben are in debate and many variations have popped up like the Rachel, Grouper, West Coast, and even a Vegas manifestation, behold the birth of Reuben, the Magnificent. Swiss cheese casts a magic spell with sautéed tempeh, sauerkraut, Thousand Island dressing, and pumpernickel to give you a new legend-in-the-making.

Preheat the oven to 400°F. In a large skillet over medium heat, combine the vegetable stock, garlic, soy sauce, and shallots. Bring just to a boil, then add the tempeh squares. Return the stock to a boil, lower the heat to simmer, cover, and cook for 20 minutes.

Toast the pumpernickel bread and generously spread one side of each slice with the Thousand Island dressing. Place four slices of the bread, dressing side up, on a baking sheet and top with the sauerkraut, Swiss cheese, and sautéed tempeh. Top with the remaining bread slices, dressing side down. Bake for 10 minutes, flipping the sandwiches after 5 minutes. Serve immediately.

yields 4 SANDWICHES

the mile-high club

This is one club that's definitely worth the climb to get into! Perfect for a tree-house powwow or poolside lunch at the Country Club, three towering levels of arugula, tomato, avocado slices, smoky or spicy hot seitan (or Tofurky drizzled with liquid smoke as pictured), and the Far East flare of mung bean sprouts provide a whirlwind of flavor.

In a medium-size bowl, combine the mayonnaise and arugula. Spread the mixture on four slices of the toasted bread.

Divide the sprouts over the mayonnaise mixture. Top each with a tomato slice and a slice of seitan. Top the seitan with another slice of toasted bread, and top that with another tomato slice, then avocado, then seitan. Place two slices of the Swiss cheese over the seitan. Spread the remaining mayonnaise mixture over the remaining four toast slices and place a toast slice over the Swiss cheese.

Cut the sandwiches into four triangles and press a toothpick into each quarter to secure the sandwich.

yields 4 SANDWICHES

1/2 CUP VEGAN MAYONNAISE (PAGE 13, OR STORE-BOUGHT, SUCH AS VEGENAISE)

1/4 CUP ROUGHLY CHOPPED ARUGULA LEAVES

12 SLICES TOASTED VEGAN SOURDOUGH BREAD

1 CUP MUNG BEAN OR ALFALFA SPROUTS

2 MEDIUM-LARGE TOMATOES, SLICED 1/4-INCH THICK (12 SLICES)

12 SANDWICH-SIZE SLICES SEITAN, EITHER MARINATED IN DROP IT LIKE IT'S HOT OR SEITAN FLARES HOT SAUCE (PAGE 12 OR 138, RESPECTIVELY) OR LIGHTLY DRIZZLED WITH LIQUID SMOKE, OR TOFURKY, LIGHTLY DRIZZLED WITH LIQUID SMOKE (OPTIONAL; SEE NOTE).

1 AVOCADO, PEELED, HALVED, PITTED, AND SLICED 1/4-INCH THICK

8 SLICES VEGAN SWISS CHEESE (PAGE 34, OR STORE-BOUGHT)

note: Tofurky products are becoming more widely available in stores. For more information, go to Tofurky.com.

the super hero

CANOLA OIL, FOR GREASING THE
BAKING SHEET

2 (8-OUNCE) PACKAGES SEITAN

1/2 CUP WALNUTS

1/2 CUP FRESH BREAD CRUMBS

3 TABLESPOONS CHOPPED FRESH BASIL

3 TABLESPOONS CHOPPED FRESH
CILANTRO LEAVES

2 TABLESPOONS EXTRA-VIRGIN OLIVE OIL

2 CLOVES GARLIC, PRESSED

1 TEASPOON VEGAN LOW-SODIUM
SOY SAUCE

1/2 TEASPOON DRIED OREGANO

1/2 TEASPOON DRIED THYME

2 TABLESPOONS TOMATO PASTE

1 (24-OUNCE) BOTTLE OF YOUR FAVORITE
VEGAN PASTA SAUCE

2 (8- TO 10-INCH) VEGAN SUBMARINE
SANDWICH LOAVES

10 SLICES VEGAN MOZZARELLA CHEESE
(PAGE 31, OR STORE-BOUGHT)

GRATED VEGAN PARMESAN CHEESE
(PAGE 39, OR STORE-BOUGHT)

note: *The seitan, walnut, and herb balls also make a sensational substitute in a number of recipes and dishes calling for traditional meatballs.*

Time to break out that red cape and golden lasso! Villainous hunger pains don't stand a chance against this fully loaded super sub. The seitan, walnut, and herb balls join forces with mozzarella and Parmesan cheese to satisfy even your biggest eaters and make the world a better place, especially at mealtime.

Preheat the oven to 400°F. Rub a baking sheet with the canola oil. Chop the seitan into 1/2-inch cubes. Transfer the cubes to a food processor and blend until crumbs form, but not until the seitan is a paste. Add the walnuts and pulse until crumbly. Transfer the mixture to a roomy bowl. Using your hands, blend in the bread crumbs, basil, cilantro, 1 tablespoon of the olive oil, and the garlic, soy sauce, oregano, thyme, and tomato paste. Mix well and shape the mixture into eighteen balls that are a little larger than golf balls.

Place the seitan balls on the greased baking sheet and brush with the remaining tablespoon of olive oil. Bake until lightly browned, about 20 minutes, turning once or twice.

Meanwhile, in a medium-size saucepan, bring the pasta sauce just to a simmer over medium heat.

Split the bread loaves and pull out some of the bread in the center of the bottoms of the loaves to make room for the meatballs. Toast the loaf halves in the hot oven for a few minutes.

Spoon a moderate amount of the hot pasta sauce into the bread canals, and spoon the meatballs over the sauce. Top the meatballs with a little more sauce, cover with the mozzarella slices, and then with the loaf tops. Slice the sandwiches in half crosswise and scatter generously with the Parmesan cheese.

yields 2 TO 4 SERVINGS

outta the park
shiitake sliders

Shiitake mushrooms have been prized in Japan for decades. Here, they hit a home run with a sensational alternative to everyday burgers. Also, transform them into Pizza Palace Sliders by adding warmed pizza sauce, maybe a few minced bell peppers or banana peppers, and exchanging the Cheddar for Parmesan or mozzarella cheese (page 39 or 31, respectively, or store-bought).

Brush the mushrooms and onion slices with the olive oil, and sprinkle them with salt and pepper.

Heat a cast-iron or grill pan over medium heat until quite hot. Carefully add the oiled mushrooms and cook until tender, about 5 to 6 minutes, turning once. Transfer the mushrooms to a plate and keep warm.

Place the onion slices in the hot pan, adding a bit of olive oil if necessary. Cook the onion for about 8 minutes, turning occasionally. Transfer the onion slices to a plate and keep warm.

Split the slider buns and toast them in the hot pan for about 2 minutes per side, or until just browned.

On a work surface, open the buns. Place a mushroom on each bun, and then cover each mushroom with an onion slice. Finish each sandwich with a slice of cheese. Close the sandwiches and serve at once.

yields 8 SLIDERS

8 SHIITAKE MUSHROOMS, STEMMED, BLACK GILLS SCRAPED AWAY

1 MEDIUM-SIZE RED ONION, CUT INTO ¼-INCH SLICES

3 TABLESPOONS EXTRA-VIRGIN OLIVE OIL, PLUS MORE, IF NEEDED, FOR THE GRILL PAN

SALT AND FRESHLY GROUND BLACK PEPPER

8 VEGAN SLIDER BUNS, OR STURDY VEGAN BREAD CUT INTO SLIDER-SIZE CIRCLES

8 SLICES VEGAN CHEDDAR, AMERICAN, WINE, JACK, OR MUENSTER CHEESE (PAGE 28, 45, 30, 42, OR 44, RESPECTIVELY, OR STORE-BOUGHT)

pita pizza in a pocket

½ CUP PREPARED VEGAN MARINARA SAUCE, POSSIBLY MORE

2 VEGAN PITA POCKET ROUNDS, SLICED IN HALF

2 CUPS GRATED VEGAN MOZZARELLA CHEESE (PAGE 31, OR STORE-BOUGHT)

FILLINGS OF CHOICE (SEE SUGGESTED FILLINGS LIST)

suggested fillings

SLICED VEGAN PIMIENTO-STUFFED GREEN OLIVES

SLICED PICKLED ARTICHOKES SPRINKLED WITH DRIED OREGANO

SLICED PICKLED JALAPEÑO PEPPERS

SLICED SAUTÉED MUSHROOMS

SLICED SAUTÉED ONIONS

SAUTÉED BROCCOLI FLORETS

SAUTÉED EGGPLANT CUBES

OTHER GRATED CHEESES FROM CHAPTER 1

The mere idea of pampering your appetite with these pita pizzas stuffed with mozzarella cheese, olives, pickled artichokes, sautéed mushrooms, onions, and whatever else you'd like is so tempting, you may throw all caution to the wind (and you should!). Also, check out the alternative Pizza Mountain Pie recipe (page 123) that lets you take this pizza party into the wilds with you.

Preheat the oven to 350°F. Generously spread the marinara sauce inside each of the four pita pockets. Stuff them with the mozzarella cheese and your selection of fillings, and place them on a baking sheet.

Bake the pita pizzas for 10 to 15 minutes, or until the cheese is starting to ooze out of the pockets. Let them cool for a few minutes before serving.

yields 2 TO 4 SERVINGS

pizza mountain pie

Inexpensive and readily available everywhere (PieIron.com is one go-to source), mountain pie makers consist of a heavy cast-iron shell that's perfect for holding two slices of bread with filling, and long steel handles with wooden grips. You can also use dessert-style fillings, such as cherry and apple. Or consider using a mountain pie maker to create outdoor versions of the grilled cheese sandwiches in this chapter.

To make one Pizza Mountain Pie: Coat one side of each slice of bread with vegan margarine. Top the uncoated side of one slice with the desired fillings, such as pizza sauce, vegan cheese or nutritional yeast, onions, bell peppers, banana peppers, mushrooms, and so on. Cover this filling or mixture with the other slice of bread, margarine-coated side facing out. Using a mountain pie maker sprayed with nonstick cooking spray, place the pie in the pie maker, and close it, locking it in place. Put the pie maker directly into red-hot coals. The cooking time will vary on the heat, so check the pie often, every few minutes, cooking until the bread is toasted and hot.

yields 1 PIZZA MOUNTAIN PIE

2 SLICES VEGAN BREAD

2 TABLESPOONS VEGAN MARGARINE

3 TABLESPOONS VEGAN PIZZA SAUCE, OR TO TASTE

½ CUP GRATED VEGAN MOZZARELLA CHEESE (PAGE 31, OR STORE-BOUGHT)

FILLINGS OF CHOICE (SEE SUGGESTED FILLINGS LIST, PAGE 122)

avocado & parmesan pita lunch rush

2 VEGAN WHOLE WHEAT PITA POCKETS

4 TABLESPOONS VEGAN MAYONNAISE
(PAGE 13, OR STORE-BOUGHT, SUCH
AS VEGENAISE)

2 RIPE AVOCADOS, PEELED, PITTED,
AND SLICED INTO 1/2-INCH WEDGES

1 RED ONION, MINCED

1 GREEN BELL PEPPER, SEEDED AND
DICED

FRESHLY GROUND BLACK PEPPER
(OPTIONAL)

4 TABLESPOONS VEGAN PARMESAN
CHEESE (PAGE 39, OR STORE-BOUGHT)

For an easy-breezy lunch on the run or anytime snack, these whole wheat pita pockets combine avocado, red onion, green bell pepper, and Parmesan cheese to redefine what a mouthwatering sandwich really is. If available, alfalfa sprouts add a whimsical flair.

Halve the pita pouches crosswise. Open them carefully, and spread 1 tablespoon of the mayonnaise into each pocket. Spoon in the avocado wedges, dividing the wedges among all four pouches. Sprinkle the minced onion liberally over the avocados, then divide the diced pepper among the pouches. Finish with pepper to taste (if using) and 1 tablespoon of the Parmesan cheese sprinkled over each pita filling.

yields 4 PITA SANDWICHES

black bean & jalapeño tacos

Time to add even more spice to taco night! Black beans play host to cumin, jalapeños, cilantro, Cheddar cheese, and Tabasco sauce to give you a stuffed tortilla you'll dream about long after the last bite.

In a medium-size skillet, combine the beans with the cumin, salt, and pepper. Cook the beans over medium heat until warmed through.

Plate the corn tortillas and spoon an adequate amount of beans into the center of each tortilla. Sprinkle with the onion, jalapeños, cilantro, and Cheddar cheese. Drizzle with Tabasco sauce, gently fold the tortillas in half, and serve at once.

yields 8 TACOS

1 (14-OUNCE) CAN BLACK BEANS, DRAINED AND RINSED

2 TEASPOONS GROUND CUMIN

SALT AND FRESHLY GROUND BLACK PEPPER

8 CORN TORTILLAS, TOASTED LIGHTLY

1 MEDIUM-SIZE WHITE ONION, DICED

2 JALAPEÑOS, STEMMED AND CHOPPED

1 BUNCH CILANTRO, LEAVES ONLY, WELL CHOPPED

1 CUP GRATED VEGAN CHEDDAR CHEESE (PAGE 28, OR STORE-BOUGHT)

TABASCO SAUCE

note: *You can use refried beans, if you wish, but check the can's label. Many brands of refried beans are made with lard.*

build your own quesadilla

8 (8- TO 10-INCH) VEGAN FLOUR
TORTILLAS

2 CUPS GRATED VEGAN JACK OR
CHEDDAR CHEESE, OR 1 CUP OF EACH,
MIXED (PAGE 42 OR 28, RESPECTIVELY,
OR STORE-BOUGHT)

FILLINGS OF CHOICE (SEE SUGGESTED
FILLINGS LIST)

HOT SAUCE, SALSA, AND/OR GUACAMOLE
OF CHOICE, FOR SERVING

suggested fillings

SLICED VEGAN PIMIENTO-STUFFED GREEN
OLIVES

SLICED PICKLED OR FRESH JALAPEÑOS

SLICED SAUTÉED MUSHROOMS

SLICED SAUTÉED ONIONS

1 RIPE TOMATO, CUT INTO ¼-INCH CUBES

1 RED BELL PEPPER, SEEDED AND CUT
INTO ¼-INCH CUBES

Quick and easy, these Mexican delights are endlessly versatile. For parties or fun family dinner nights, set up a Build Your Own Quesadilla bar by placing fillings of choice in separate clear glass bowls for everyone to choose from. Plus, a nearby bottle of tequila, surrounded by shot glasses, for impulsive toasts will add a certain exclamation point of authenticity.

Place two dry 10-inch cast-iron skillets over medium heat. When the skillets are hot, place a flour tortilla in each. Toast for 1 to 2 minutes, until the tortillas just start to brown. Turn the tortillas with tongs, sprinkle an adequate amount of cheese on each tortilla, and add the fillings of choice. Then cover each with another tortilla. After 1 to 2 minutes, carefully turn the tortillas with the tongs or a spatula. Toast for another 1 to 2 minutes, or until the tortillas are tanned on the turned side and the cheese has melted. Repeat with the remaining tortillas and cheese, adjusting the heat if necessary. Serve with your choice of hot sauce, salsa, and/or guacamole.

yields 4 QUESADILLAS

cool as a cucumber finger sandwiches

These blast-from-the-past teatime (or cocktail hour) sandwiches are back to feed a new generation. They aim to please whether you're one of the ladies and gents who lunch, or facing a kitchen full of kiddies who have the afterschool munchies.

Slice the bread and cut it into 3-inch squares. Spread each square with margarine. Spread an ample amount of the cream cheese on each cucumber slice, and place a cucumber slice on each buttered bread square. Sprinkle generously with minced dill. Close the sandwiches and serve.

yields 6 TO 8 SERVINGS

1 LOAF VEGAN BROWN BREAD

4 TABLESPOONS (1/2 STICK) VEGAN MARGARINE, AT ROOM TEMPERATURE

8 OUNCES VEGAN CREAM CHEESE, SOFTENED (PAGE 37, OR STORE-BOUGHT)

1 MEDIUM-SIZE CUCUMBER, PEELED, SEEDED, AND SLICED INTO 1/4-INCH ROUNDS

1/3 CUP MINCED FRESH DILL

lulu's finger sandwiches

2 CUPS CUBED VEGAN CHEDDAR CHEESE
(PAGE 28, OR STORE-BOUGHT)

3 SHALLOTS, PEELED AND QUARTERED

1 (4-OUNCE) BOTTLE PIMIENTOS, WELL
DRAINED

½ CUP VEGAN KETCHUP

½ TO 1 TEASPOON DRY MUSTARD,
SUCH AS COLMAN'S

1 TABLESPOON CHILI SAUCE

1 CUP VEGAN MAYONNAISE (PAGE 13,
OR STORE-BOUGHT, SUCH AS VEGENAISE)

TABASCO SAUCE

8 TO 10 SLICES VEGAN WHOLE WHEAT
BREAD, CRUSTS REMOVED, TOASTED AND
CUT INTO QUARTERS

I do declare! Lulu Paste is as Southern as Ms. O'Hara herself. A tray of these finger sandwiches, spread with a Cheddar cheese, shallot, pimiento, and chili sauce mixture, is mighty tasty with a round of mint juleps served on the front porch. Speaking of which, when you add Lulu's Front Porch Juleps (see recipe that follows on page 132), every bite *and* sip will be Derby Day.

In a food processor, combine the Cheddar cheese, shallots, and pimientos. Process until very smooth. Add the ketchup, dry mustard, chili sauce, mayonnaise, and Tabasco sauce. Process again for 1 to 2 minutes.

Arrange the toast slices on a work surface. Spread half the slices gently with the Lulu Paste, top with the remaining slices, and serve.

yields 4 TO 5 SANDWICHES

lulu's front porch juleps

15 TO 20 OUNCES BOURBON

35 FRESH MINT LEAVES, WASHED AND
DRIED, PLUS 10 TO 12 FRESH MINT SPRIGS
FOR SERVING

1 CUP VEGAN SUGAR

1 CUP WATER

Historically served in silver or pewter cups and held by the bottom or rim, feel free to buck tradition by serving these minty juleps however, and whenever, you wish. They especially pair nicely with Lulu's Finger Sandwiches (page 130).

In a small bowl, soak the mint leaves in about 3 ounces of the bourbon for 1 hour. Meanwhile, in a small saucepan, create a simple syrup by combining the sugar and water and stirring the mixture constantly over medium heat until the sugar is dissolved, 4 to 5 minutes.

In a clear glass container with a lid, combine the minted bourbon and simple syrup. Chill, covered, in the refrigerator overnight.

To serve: Use julep cups (preferably the traditional silver, but any favorite 10- to 12-ounce glass will do). Fill the cups with crushed ice and insert a fresh mint sprig. Pour 1 ounce of the remaining straight bourbon into each cup, followed by the minted bourbon.

yields 10 TO 12 SERVINGS

smoked seitan & avocado panini

Italian ciabatta, avocado, mayonnaise, and smoky seitan make these panini so messy-delicious, and quite filling. Fear not if you don't have a panini press: Either use this as your excuse to get one or simply use two cast-iron skillets (one fitting inside the other). Also, trade in the smoky flavor to make Red Hot Seitan & Avocado Panini by marinating the seitan in Frank's Red Hot Cayenne Pepper Sauce, Drop It Like It's Hot (page 12), or the Seitan Flares Hot Sauce (page 138).

Trim off the ends from the ciabatta and cut it in half crosswise. Slice each half down the middle lengthwise. Spread 1 tablespoon of the olive oil on the cut side of two slices, invert the slices over their partner slices, and "share" the olive oil. Place all four slices, oiled side down, on waxed paper on a cutting board.

Heat a panini press to high heat, or heat two cast-iron skillets over medium heat until fairly hot.

Peel, halve, and pit the avocado and cut it into eight slices. Spread the mayonnaise on the crusty sides of the two "flat" ciabatta slices and give them a good grinding of black pepper. Divide the Swiss cheese slices over two of the slices, place the avocado slices on the Swiss cheese, and top with the seitan slices.

Close the sandwiches and place them in the hot panini press or between the hot skillets. Close the panini press lid and press with the handle for 30 seconds. Grill until there are nice brown grill marks all over the bread, 3 to 4 minutes. Serve at once with a sharp knife and fork.

yields 2 LARGE PANINI

1 VEGAN CIABATTA, NOT TOO THICK, ABOUT 1 FOOT LONG BY 6 INCHES WIDE

2 TO 4 TABLESPOONS EXTRA-VIRGIN OLIVE OIL

1 RIPE AVOCADO

VEGAN MAYONNAISE (PAGE 13, OR STORE-BOUGHT, SUCH AS VEGENAISE)

FRESHLY GROUND BLACK PEPPER

4 (¼-INCH) SLICES VEGAN SWISS CHEESE (PAGE 34, OR STORE-BOUGHT)

½ POUND SLICED SEITAN, DRIZZLED VERY LIGHTLY WITH LIQUID SMOKE

CHAPTER 6

Appetizers & Snacks

It would be hard to imagine any occasion, from a cozy night on the couch, after-school snack time, or small family get-together to a larger holiday celebration where cheese is not on the table somewhere. In fact, usually it's *everywhere!* From dips to finger foods, cheese dominates, but until now, it has left most of us empty-handed and hungry.

On the following pages, we once more infuse the "happy" back into a family-friendly snack time or happy hour with such dips as Blue Moon, Flying Buffalo, Amazo-Queso, Cheddar Pub, and Crunchy Leek. And get ready to behold Cheesy Hummus with such additional offerings as Blue Cheese Hummus, Hot Pepper Cheese Hummus, and Smoky Cheese Hummus. Some of the dips use the homemade cheeses from Chapter 1; others inventively spin a lineup of everyday ingredients into the cheesy flavors and texture we've so longed for.

This lineup continues with everyday treats that light up and fire up the taste buds. Finger-licking quick bites such as the Dynamic Jalapeño Popper Duo, Cheddar Chips, Fried Olives Stuffed with Smoky Cheese Hummus, Swiss Mangoes, White Truffle Rice-Stuffed Mushrooms, and Parmesan Popcorn all prove to be guaranteed good mood food.

blue moon dip

1 CUP VEGAN MAYONNAISE (PAGE 13, OR STORE-BOUGHT, SUCH AS VEGENAISE)

½ TEASPOON GARLIC POWDER

½ TEASPOON ONION POWDER

½ TEASPOON TAHINI

1 TEASPOON FRESHLY SQUEEZED LIME JUICE

1 TEASPOON CIDER VINEGAR

¼ CUP EXTRA-FIRM TOFU, PRESSED AND DRAINED (SEE PAGE 18)

This dip not only comes very close to tasting like its dairy doppelgänger, it blows right on by it. Serve with your favorite selection of cut vegetables, such as carrots, celery, cauliflower, broccoli, and cucumbers, or potato chips and pretzels. Or serve it alongside spicy-hot dishes, such as Flying Buffalo Dip (page 144) or Seitan Flares (see recipe that follows on page 138), which are making a special cameo here from *Grilling Vegan Style*.

In a large bowl, mix the mayonnaise, garlic powder, onion powder, tahini, lime juice, and cider vinegar. When well blended, crumble the tofu into small lumps with your hands and stir it into the mayonnaise mixture. Let the mixture rest for 15 minutes or more before serving.

yields 4 TO 6 SERVINGS

seitan flares

1 POUND SEITAN, TORN OR CUT INTO CHUNKS LARGE ENOUGH TO FIT LOOSELY ON THE GRILL GRATE, OR SKEWERED

EXTRA-VIRGIN OLIVE OIL

hot sauce

¼ CUP OF YOUR FAVORITE HOT SAUCE, FRANK'S RED HOT CAYENNE PEPPER SAUCE PREFERRED

3 TABLESPOONS PURE MAPLE SYRUP

¼ CUP FRESHLY SQUEEZED LIME JUICE

½ TEASPOON SALT

CAYENNE PEPPER (THE MORE, THE HOTTER!)

2 TABLESPOONS CHOPPED FRESH OREGANO (OPTIONAL)

note: *This dish can also be prepared using a grill pan or skillet over a stove instead of a grill. Also, instead of preparing the following hot sauce, feel free to substitute Drop It Like It's Hot (page 12).*

If you like hot wings, this grilled version made with seitan boasts the same texture and *knock you on your ass* flavors as good as regular hot wings, especially when you pile on the cayenne pepper. These Seitan Flares are making a special appearance here from *Grilling Vegan Style* to accompany the Blue Moon Dip (page 136).

Heat the grill to medium high.

Marinate the seitan in the olive oil to cover for 1 hour. Grill the seitan until lightly browned, 3 to 5 minutes or longer, turning often. Transfer to a bowl.

Meanwhile, in a glass measuring cup, whisk together the hot sauce, maple syrup, lime juice, salt, and cayenne pepper to taste. Microwave the mixture on high for 1 minute or until fairly hot, or whisk the mixture together in a small saucepan and place it over direct heat on the grill until it is hot, 4 to 5 minutes or longer, depending on the grill. Add the mixture to the seitan bowl and stir gently to combine, or coat the seitan if it is skewered. Finish with the oregano (if using).

Alternatively, marinate the seitan in the Drop It Like It's Hot sauce for several hours to overnight. Arrange the seitan on skewers, if desired, and place on the grill for 6 to 8 minutes, turning often, or until browned. Continue to brush on the hot sauce. Serve with extra sauce and celery sticks.

yields 4 SERVINGS

crunchy leek dip

Thanks to the water chestnuts, this leek dip, made with cottage cheese, has a crunch*tastic* texture. In fact, it's such a favorite for any occasion that I've never had so much as a teaspoon of it left over.

In a large bowl, blend the mayonnaise with the cottage cheese, leek soup mix, water chestnuts, and spinach. Chill the mixture in the refrigerator overnight.

When you're ready to serve, slice off the top of the sourdough loaf and scoop out the bread inside, leaving about a 1-inch margin of bread all the way around the inner crust. Tear the scooped bread into chunks for dipping. Fill the scooped loaf with the chilled dip.

yields 6 TO 8 SERVINGS

2 CUPS VEGAN MAYONNAISE (PAGE 13, OR STORE-BOUGHT, SUCH AS VEGENAISE)

1 CUP VEGAN COTTAGE CHEESE (PAGE 36, OR STORE-BOUGHT)

2 OUNCES VEGAN DRY LEEK SOUP MIX

6 OUNCES CANNED WATER CHESTNUTS, DRAINED AND CHOPPED ROUGHLY

6 OUNCES FROZEN CHOPPED SPINACH, THAWED AND DRAINED THOROUGHLY

1 ROUND LOAF VEGAN SOURDOUGH BREAD

the sailor's spinach dip

Popeye would be in love! You may think you know spinach dip, but wait until you get a mouthful of this one. This robust dip with its additional thicker, baked option will carry you and your guests through any occasion, from game night with the kids to poker night with your buddies, or sailing on the high seas in search of adventure.

In a dry cast-iron skillet, toss the cashews over medium-high heat until fragrant and lightly toasted. Transfer the cashews to a bowl, and pour in the vegetable stock and white rum. Let the cashews soak for ½ hour, to soften them for blending, then drain the cashews.

In a food processor, combine the spinach, garlic powder, onion powder, lime juice, and vinegar. Pulse for 30 to 40 seconds, then pour in the cashews and pulse until well blended. Taste carefully, and add salt and pepper to taste.

Serve with the carrot and celery sticks, toast points, and/or rice crackers.

For a thicker version, bake in a preheated 300ºF oven for 10 to 15 minutes.

yields ABOUT 5 CUPS DIP

1 CUP RAW, UNSALTED CASHEWS

½ CUP VEGAN VEGETABLE STOCK

½ CUP WHITE RUM, OR 1 CUP VEGETABLE STOCK

1 POUND FROZEN SPINACH, THAWED, DRAINED, AND PRESSED BETWEEN LAYERS OF PAPER TOWELS TO REMOVE EXTRA MOISTURE

1 TABLESPOON GARLIC POWDER

1 TABLESPOON ONION POWDER

¼ CUP FRESHLY SQUEEZED LIME JUICE

1 TABLESPOON CIDER VINEGAR

SALT AND FRESHLY GROUND BLACK PEPPER

CARROT AND CELERY STICKS, FOR SERVING

VEGAN TOAST POINTS, FOR SERVING

SMALL VEGAN RICE CRACKERS, FOR SERVING

amazo-queso dip

Friday nights were practically invented for this Mexican-inspired Cheddar cheese dip! Cashews, oatmeal, and a spirited mixture of spices recharge this versatile dip, which works alone with tortilla chips or as an ingredient in such dishes as the Minced Chipotle Pepper & Cheese Dip (page 149) and Smoky Cheese Hummus (page 152).

In a blender or food processor, combine the cashews, oatmeal, water, onion powder, garlic powder, and turmeric. Puree until the mixture is smooth. It may seem thin, but it will thicken in due course.

Pour the mixture into a sturdy saucepan and place over medium-low heat, stirring often to prevent sticking. Add the tomatoes with their liquid, or the salsa (if using), Cheddar cheese, paprika, hot peppers, chili powder, and cayenne pepper, and stir to combine. Taste the mixture and add salt and pepper to taste. Cook the mixture, stirring regularly, until you reach the texture you want. You can add a bit more water if it gets too thick.

yields 6 SERVINGS

½ CUP RAW, UNSALTED CASHEWS, SOAKED IN CANNED VEGAN VEGETABLE STOCK FOR 90 MINUTES, DRAINED

½ CUP RAW OATMEAL, GROUND INTO POWDER

1½ CUPS BOTTLED WATER

2 TEASPOONS ONION POWDER

1 TEASPOON GARLIC POWDER

½ TEASPOON GROUND TURMERIC

14 OUNCES CANNED DICED ORGANIC TOMATOES OR MEDIUM-HOT SALSA

½ CUP GRATED VEGAN CHEDDAR CHEESE (PAGE 28, OR STORE-BOUGHT)

1 TEASPOON SMOKED SPANISH PAPRIKA

2 TEASPOONS FINELY MINCED PICKLED HOT PEPPERS, OR TO TASTE

½ TEASPOON CHILI POWDER

PINCH OF CAYENNE PEPPER, OR TO TASTE

SALT AND FRESHLY GROUND BLACK PEPPER

cheddar pub dip

With its time-honored pairing of Cheddar cheese and beer plus a few unique twists, this is an ultimate party dip. It's also an irresistibly tangy spread on baguette slices with chutney and diced tomatoes.

In a food processor, combine the Cheddar cheese with the beer, garlic powder, onion powder, mustard, and cayenne pepper, and blend until smooth. Season the beer cheese with salt and white pepper.

Serve as a dip with pretzels.

Or to make Cheddar Pub Baguettes: Place a rack 6 inches below the broiler and heat the broiler for a good 10 to 15 minutes. Spread the baguette slices (if using) with the beer cheese and arrange them on a rimmed baking sheet. Broil for about 2 minutes, rotating the pan, until the cheese is bubbling and the bread and cheese are browning around the edges. Spread lightly with the chutney (if using), top with the tomatoes (if using), and serve at once. Or serve the Cheddar Pub Baguettes with a soup and/or salad from Chapter 3.

yields 6 TO 8 SERVINGS

2 CUPS (1-INCH-CUBED) VEGAN EXTRA-SHARP CHEDDAR CHEESE (PAGE 28, OR STORE-BOUGHT)

¾ CUP DARK BEER OR STOUT

2 TEASPOONS GARLIC POWDER

1 TEASPOON ONION POWDER

1 TABLESPOON VEGAN DIJON MUSTARD, OR TO TASTE

½ TEASPOON CAYENNE PEPPER, OR MORE TO TASTE

½ TEASPOON SALT, OR MORE TO TASTE

½ TEASPOON FRESHLY GROUND WHITE PEPPER, OR MORE TO TASTE

2 VEGAN BAGUETTES, CUT INTO ¼- TO ½-INCH SLICES (OPTIONAL)

PREPARED HOT CHUTNEY (OPTIONAL)

DICED TOMATOES (OPTIONAL)

flying buffalo dip

12 OUNCES EXTRA-FIRM TOFU, PRESSED AND DRAINED (SEE PAGE 18), OR SEITAN, SLICED INTO ½-INCH CUBES

1 CUP FINELY SHREDDED VEGAN CHEDDAR CHEESE (PAGE 28, OR STORE-BOUGHT)

½ CUP VEGAN MAYONNAISE (PAGE 13, OR STORE-BOUGHT, SUCH AS VEGENAISE)

1 TABLESPOON FRESHLY SQUEEZED LEMON JUICE

2 TEASPOONS CIDER VINEGAR

½ TEASPOON GARLIC POWDER

½ TEASPOON ONION POWDER

SALT AND FRESHLY GROUND BLACK PEPPER

3 TABLESPOONS FRANK'S RED HOT CAYENNE PEPPER SAUCE, OR TO TASTE

TOASTED VEGAN PITA TRIANGLES, FOR SERVING

Game day is calling and it wants a Buffalo "wing" dip *everyone* can enjoy! In addition to serving this blazing dip alone with toasted pita triangles, another option is to serve it alongside homemade Blue Cheese Dressing (page 41) or Blue Moon Dip (page 136) with celery sticks for dipping.

In a large bowl, combine the tofu, Cheddar cheese, mayonnaise, lemon juice, vinegar, garlic powder, onion powder, salt, pepper, and hot sauce. Mix well, and serve warm or at room temperature with toasted pita triangles.

yields 6 TO 8 SERVINGS

lucky horseradish dip

1½ CUPS FINELY SHREDDED VEGAN
HORSERADISH AMERICAN OR
HORSERADISH CHEDDAR CHEESE
(PAGE 45 OR 28, RESPECTIVELY,
OR STORE-BOUGHT)

3 TABLESPOONS VEGAN KETCHUP

2 TABLESPOONS VEGAN
WORCESTERSHIRE SAUCE (PAGE 23,
OR STORE-BOUGHT)

1 TABLESPOON VEGAN HORSERADISH
SAUCE, OR TO TASTE (OPTIONAL,
IF TOO STRONG)

1 TABLESPOON WHITE RUM (OPTIONAL)

SALT AND FRESHLY GROUND BLACK
PEPPER

This fiery little treat is ready in a few minutes, but let it rest for at least a half hour before serving to let the flavors of Horseradish American Cheese, ketchup, and Worcestershire sauce blend. This dip is a particularly lucky bet with French fries or fried onion rings.

In a small bowl, mix all the ingredients. Let the mixture rest, then serve with crackers or vegetables, or French fries and onion rings.

yields 2½ CUPS

avocado, corn & black bean dip

As if it's not already yummy enough, you can further amp up this colorful blend of avocado, corn, black beans, and Parmesan cheese by using medium-hot prepared salsa and even carefully stirring in some ground cayenne pepper.

In a large bowl, combine the avocados, corn, beans, red onion, salsa, cilantro, and lime juice. Toss well, then add the chili powder, Parmesan cheese, salt, and black pepper, and mix again. Serve with the tortilla chips.

yields 10 TO 12 SERVINGS

2 RIPE AVOCADOS, PEELED, HALVED, PITTED, AND DICED

1½ CUPS FROZEN CORN KERNELS, THAWED

1 (14-OUNCE) CAN BLACK BEANS, DRAINED AND RINSED

1 MEDIUM-SIZE RED ONION, MINCED

1 CUP PREPARED SALSA, PREFERABLY MEDIUM-SPICED

2 TABLESPOONS CHOPPED FRESH CILANTRO LEAVES

JUICE OF 1 LIME

2 TABLESPOONS CHILI POWDER

¼ CUP GRATED VEGAN PARMESAN CHEESE (PAGE 39, OR STORE-BOUGHT)

SALT AND FRESHLY GROUND BLACK PEPPER

PLENTY OF VEGAN TORTILLA CHIPS, FOR SERVING

minced chipotle pepper & cheese dip

You can temper the sizzle in this dip by adding more (!!!) or less of the adobo with which the chipotle peppers are canned.

In a large serving bowl, place the Amazo-Queso Dip. Add the chipotles, olives, and capers to the bowl and stir well. Sprinkle the lime juice over the mixture and stir again. Taste carefully, and add the reserved adobo to taste if you want more heat. Serve at room temperature with the tortilla chips.

yields 8 TO 10 SERVINGS

1 RECIPE AMAZO-QUESO DIP (PAGE 142)

1 (7½-OUNCE) CAN CHIPOTLE PEPPERS IN ADOBO, DRAINED, STEMMED, AND MINCED FINELY, ADOBO RESERVED

15 SMALL VEGAN GREEN OLIVES STUFFED WITH PIMIENTOS, MINCED FINELY

2 TABLESPOONS BOTTLED CAPERS, DRAINED WELL AND CHOPPED

1 TABLESPOON FRESHLY SQUEEZED LIME JUICE

VEGAN TORTILLA CHIPS, FOR SERVING

fried olives stuffed with smoky cheese hummus

1 TEASPOON MINCED FRESH ROSEMARY LEAVES

2 SAGE LEAVES, MINCED

1 RECIPE SMOKY CHEESE HUMMUS (PAGE 152)

24 PITTED SPANISH OLIVES, PATTED DRY

PEANUT OIL, FOR FRYING

ALL-PURPOSE FLOUR

¾ CUP VEGAN EGG REPLACER

1 CUP FINE DRY VEGAN BREAD CRUMBS

Smoky Cheese Hummus matched with Spanish olives makes this an unusual and addictive way to treat olives. And, while we're on the topic, check out the instructions for creating Casanova's Blue Cheese- or Feta-Stuffed Cocktail Olives (page 153) for all those dirty martinis, salads, artisanal platters, snacks, and more.

In a large bowl, combine the rosemary and sage with the Smoky Cheese Hummus. Place the mixture in a resealable plastic bag. Snip off a corner and pipe the hummus mixture into each pitted olive. Let the olives rest for 15 minutes.

In a medium-size skillet over medium-high heat, bring the peanut oil to 350°F. When a pinch of flour sizzles in the oil, it's ready.

Toss the stuffed olives with flour, then dip each olive into the egg replacer, then into the dry bread crumbs. Fry the olives until golden brown, 30 to 45 seconds. With a slotted spoon, transfer the fried olives to paper towels to drain. Serve hot.

yields 24 STUFFED OLIVES

cheesy hummus

1 CUP RAW, UNSALTED CASHEWS

¾ CUP CANNED VEGAN VEGETABLE STOCK

2 TEASPOONS GARLIC POWDER

2 TEASPOONS ONION POWDER

JUICE OF 1 LARGE LEMON

½ CUP NUTRITIONAL YEAST

1 CUP CANNED CHICKPEAS, RINSED AND WELL DRAINED

2 TABLESPOONS TAHINI

1 TEASPOON SALT, OR TO TASTE

1 TEASPOON CHILI POWDER, PLUS MORE FOR GARNISHING

1 TEASPOON DRIED OREGANO

2 TEASPOONS MINCED FRESH CHIVES

1 TEASPOON MINCED FRESH DILL (OPTIONAL)

EXTRA-VIRGIN OLIVE OIL, FOR DRIZZLING

TOASTED VEGAN PITA TRIANGLES

This Cheesy Hummus with its blue cheese, spicy, and smoked variations is one stop shopping for your everyday snack fix. I even like to spread it on sandwiches for an added pop of flavor. You'd best get used to the title "Hummus Connoisseur," because you are about to own it big-time when you start playing around with this lip-smacking array.

In a food processor, place the cashews and pulse until fine crumbs are formed, but not until the cashews become paste. Add the stock, garlic powder, onion powder, lemon juice, nutritional yeast, chickpeas, tahini, salt, chili powder, oregano, chives, and dill (if using). Pulse until you reach your desired consistency.

Transfer the hummus to a bowl and drizzle with olive oil. Sprinkle with chili powder, and serve with pita triangles.

yields 6 SERVINGS

variations

Blue Cheese Hummus: Stir in ⅓ cup of bottled vegan blue cheese salad dressing. Or use ⅓ cup of vegan blue cheese (page 41, or store-bought) if you want the texture to be a little chunkier.

Hot Pepper Cheese Hummus: Stir in 1 to 2 tablespoons of minced jalapeños and/or habaneros. Careful with the habaneros! Then stir in about ½ cup (or to taste) of Cheddar and/or Jack cheese (page 28 or 42, respectively, or store-bought).

Smoky Cheese Hummus: Stir in ½ cup of Amazo-Queso Dip (page 142) and 1 to 2 teaspoons of liquid smoke. Or stir in ½ cup of smoked Cheddar cheese (page 28, or store-bought).

casanova's blue cheese– or feta-stuffed cocktail olives

Now you can play matchmaker, giving dirty martinis, salads, and artisanal platters the homemade blue cheese- or feta-stuffed olives they've been pining for. Or, go solo and enjoy these zesty little gems all by yourself as a snack anytime you wish.

Blend together the softened blue cheese and soy milk, until you have a texture that you can pipe into the olives. Place the mixture in a resealable plastic bag. Snip off a corner and pipe the cheese mixture into the olives.

yields 24 STUFFED OLIVES

1/2 CUP VEGAN BLUE OR FETA CHEESE (PAGE 41 OR 35, RESPECTIVELY, OR STORE-BOUGHT), SOFTENED

2 TO 3 TABLESPOONS SOY MILK

24 PITTED OLIVES

primo-pimiento spread

This lively spread made with Cheddar cheese, roasted red peppers, and other catchy flavors is ideal on toasted baguette slices, to add zest to cocktail hour or simply to serve with pretzels to satisfy afterschool or midnight munchies.

In a large bowl, combine the Cheddar cheese, red pepper, mayonnaise, beer, garlic powder, onion powder, mustard, and cayenne pepper. Stir to mix well. Season to taste with salt and white pepper. Serve at room temperature. Keeps for up to 5 days, refrigerated.

yields 8 TO 10 SERVINGS

2 CUPS FINELY GRATED VEGAN EXTRA-SHARP CHEDDAR CHEESE (PAGE 28, OR STORE-BOUGHT)

1 CUP HOMEMADE OR BOTTLED DICED ROASTED RED PEPPERS

1/2 CUP VEGAN MAYONNAISE (PAGE 13, OR STORE-BOUGHT, SUCH AS VEGENAISE)

3/4 CUP DARK BEER, STOUT, OR VEGAN VEGETABLE STOCK

2 TEASPOONS GARLIC POWDER

1 TEASPOON ONION POWDER

1 TABLESPOON VEGAN DIJON MUSTARD

1/2 TEASPOON CAYENNE PEPPER, OR MORE TO TASTE

1/2 TEASPOON SALT, OR MORE TO TASTE

1/2 TEASPOON FRESHLY GROUND WHITE PEPPER, OR MORE TO TASTE

the dynamic jalapeño popper duo

When appetites flare, make plenty of these hot poppers, offered here in two sizzling versions. First up are the Inferno Poppers that will leave your eyes watering for joy! Next are the Fiery Poppers with an accompanying spicy tomato-chipotle dipping sauce. Make one or both and you'll keep everyone happily filled to the brim with an explosion of flavor no matter the occasion.

inferno poppers

16 MEDIUM TO MEDIUM-LARGE JALAPEÑOS (SEE NOTE)

2 CUPS FINELY GRATED VEGAN JACK, AMERICAN, OR MUENSTER CHEESE (PAGE 42, 44, OR 45, RESPECTIVELY, OR STORE-BOUGHT)

FINELY CHOPPED HOT CHILE PEPPERS, SUCH AS SERRANO OR HABANERO

FRESHLY GROUND BLACK PEPPER

1 CUP VEGAN EGG REPLACER

1½ CUPS ALL-PURPOSE FLOUR

1 CUP DRY VEGAN BREAD CRUMBS OR PANKO

1½ QUARTS CANOLA OIL, FOR DEEP FRYING

note: *For those who like their jalapeño poppers with a little extra sizzle, look for jalapeños with white streaks, called striations, instead of smooth, firm peppers. You see, these hot temptresses have to stay on the plant until they mature to get the full heat in their white inner ribs (where the heat is), not in the seeds. The striations indicate that the pepper was ripened on the plant, and will therefore likely be pretty hot. That said, the only truly reliable way to determine a jalapeño's heat is to be courageous and taste a thin slice. Some people can smell the heat, but I've been fooled a few times by that method. Another solution is to use habanero and/or serrano chiles in addition to jalapeños; that way, you get the jalapeño flavor and some serious heat.*

inferno poppers

Line a baking sheet with waxed paper. With a sharp paring knife, make a lengthwise slit into each jalapeño. Wearing a finger cot or rubber gloves, work out as many seeds from the jalapeños as you can.

In a medium-size bowl, mix the Jack cheese with the chiles. Pipe or spoon this mixture into the jalapeños, placing them on the prepared baking sheet as they are stuffed. Give the stuffed peppers a good grinding of black pepper.

Put the egg replacer, flour, and bread crumbs into three separate small bowls. Dip the stuffed jalapeños first into the egg replacer, then into the flour, making sure they are well coated with each. Do not dip yet into the bread crumbs. Return the coated jalapeños to the waxed paper and let them dry for about 10 minutes.

Dip the jalapeños in the egg replacer again, and (bypassing the flour this time) roll them through the bread crumbs, making sure to coat the entire surface of the jalapeño. Let them dry on the waxed paper again for 10 minutes.

Heat the oil to 365°F. Deep-fry the coated jalapeños for 2 to 3 minutes each, until golden brown. Remove the peppers from the hot oil and let them drain in the deep-fry basket or on a paper towel.

yields 16 JALAPEÑO POPPERS

fiery poppers with tomato-chipotle sauce

Slit each jalapeño lengthwise along one side from tip to stem end and remove the seeds. Be careful to keep the bodies of the peppers intact. In a medium-size bowl, toss the Cheddar cheese with the cumin, and then stuff it into the jalapeños, pressing each slit around the cheese (the cheese will bulge out of the slit).

Put the flour, soy milk, and bread crumbs into three separate small bowls. Stir the oregano, black pepper, and salt into the bread crumbs. Dip each jalapeño in the flour, then in the soy milk, and then in the seasoned bread crumbs. Be careful to cover each pepper completely, leaving no bit of pepper or cheese uncovered.

Heat the oil to 375°F and fry the peppers, three or four at a time, until golden brown, about 1½ minutes. Drain briefly on paper towels and serve at once with Tomato-Chipotle Sauce.

yields 4 SERVINGS

tomato-chipotle sauce

Finely dice the green pepper and onion, and sauté them in the oil. Add the garlic, salt, and pepper. Add the tomatoes and chipotles and simmer very briefly. Serve in ramekins as a dipping sauce.

fiery poppers with tomato-chipotle sauce

16 LARGE FRESH JALAPEÑOS (SEE NOTE ON PAGE 156)

1 CUP FINELY GRATED VEGAN CHEDDAR, WINE, OR JACK CHEESE (PAGE 28, 30, OR 42, RESPECTIVELY, OR STORE-BOUGHT)

1 TABLESPOON GROUND CUMIN

2 CUPS ALL-PURPOSE FLOUR

1½ CUPS SOY MILK

3 CUPS DRY BREAD CRUMBS

1 TEASPOON DRIED OREGANO

1 TEASPOON FRESHLY GROUND BLACK PEPPER

1½ TEASPOONS SALT

4 CUPS CANOLA OIL

TOMATO-CHIPOTLE SAUCE (RECIPE FOLLOWS)

tomato-chipotle sauce

1 SMALL GREEN BELL PEPPER, SEEDED

1 SMALL ONION

2 TABLESPOONS CANOLA OIL

1 LARGE CLOVE GARLIC, PRESSED

SALT AND FRESHLY GROUND BLACK PEPPER

1 (14-OUNCE) CAN DICED TOMATOES, WITH THE JUICE

3 CANNED CHIPOTLE PEPPERS, STEMMED AND CHOPPED FINELY

'tis the season fruit & nut ball

2 CUPS VEGAN CREAM CHEESE (PAGE 37, OR STORE-BOUGHT), SOFTENED

1 CUP CHOPPED DRIED DATES

1 CUP TOASTED COCONUT

1 CUP RAISINS, BLACK AND WHITE, MIXED

JUICE OF 1 LEMON

2 TEASPOONS VANILLA EXTRACT

1 TEASPOON ALMOND EXTRACT

2 TEASPOONS WHITE RUM (OPTIONAL)

1 CUP CHOPPED MIXED NUTS

2 VEGAN BAGUETTES, SLICED AND TOASTED LIGHTLY

note: *The mixture must be refrigerated for a few hours to overnight, so plan accordingly.*

No need to wait for the holidays to present family and friends with this festive appetizer that proves it's always the season for fun and laughter. Homemade cream cheese serves as a base for a rolled mixture of dried dates, toasted coconut, raisins, vanilla and almond extracts, and chopped nuts.

In a large bowl and using your hands, mix the cream cheese with the dates, coconut, raisins, lemon juice, vanilla extract, almond extract, and white rum (if using). Let the mixture rest for 15 or 20 minutes to let the flavors meld.

Divide the mixture in half, then form into two large balls. Wrap the balls in waxed paper or plastic wrap and place in the refrigerator overnight, or in the freezer for a few hours. Place the mixed nuts on a sheet of waxed paper, roll each cheese ball in the chopped nuts, transfer to two roomy plates, and serve surrounded by toasted baguette slices.

yields 10 TO 12 APPETIZER SERVINGS

toasted coconut

Place an empty stainless steel skillet over medium heat. After 4 to 5 minutes, sprinkle ¾ cup of shredded coconut into the skillet. Shake the skillet every 10 seconds until the coconut has begun to brown lightly. Stir well and transfer the coconut to a medium bowl.

pecan & cranberry party log

Cashews pureed with olive oil, coconut oil, and lemon form the base for this cheese log that turns every bite into a holiday. The dried cranberry and pecan crust not only add layers of flavor but also texture and crunch.

Soak the raw cashews overnight in water to cover. When you're ready to proceed, drain the cashews and rinse them well.

In a food processor, puree the cashews, olive oil, coconut oil, lemon zest, lemon juice, tahini, salt, and about 2 tablespoons of water until smooth. You may need to add a little more water, but don't add too much.

Line a strainer with two layers of cheesecloth and place it over a large bowl. With a rubber spatula, scrape the cashew blend out of the processor bowl onto the cheesecloth. Fold the cheesecloth over the cashew mixture, covering it completely, and press to begin draining the cashew mixture. Let the mixture stand at room temperature overnight or for at least 12 hours.

Preheat the oven to 200°F. Discard the liquid from the bowl. Line a baking sheet with parchment paper. Unwrap the cashew mixture and place it on a fresh sheet of cheesecloth. Wrap the mixture and shape it into a log shape, twisting both ends of the cheesecloth to retain the shape. Transfer to the prepared baking sheet and bake for 35 to 40 minutes, turning every 10 minutes, until the log is set on the outside but still soft. Let the log cool in its wrapping, then chill in the refrigerator for at least 3 hours.

In a medium-size bowl, stir together the pecans and cranberries. When the log has firmed up, unwrap it and gently roll it in the mixture until it's covered, pressing to make the mixture adhere to the log while it retains its shape. Wrap the log in waxed paper or plastic wrap and transfer it to the refrigerator. Chill until you're ready to serve, surrounded by whole wheat crackers.

yields ABOUT 1 DOZEN APPETIZER SERVINGS

1½ CUPS RAW, UNSALTED CASHEWS

½ CUP EXTRA-VIRGIN OLIVE OIL

½ CUP COCONUT OIL

½ TEASPOON FRESHLY GRATED LEMON ZEST

½ CUP FRESHLY SQUEEZED LEMON JUICE, FROM ABOUT 2 LARGE LEMONS

2 TABLESPOONS TAHINI

1 TABLESPOON SALT, OR MORE, TO TASTE

2 TABLESPOONS WATER, PLUS MORE IF NEEDED

½ CUP CHOPPED TOASTED PECANS (SEE INSTRUCTIONS ON PAGE 212)

½ CUP CHOPPED DRIED CRANBERRIES

note: *This recipe requires overnight preparations, so plan accordingly.*

white truffle rice-stuffed mushrooms

20 MEDIUM-SIZE WHITE MUSHROOMS

SALT AND FRESHLY GROUND WHITE PEPPER

2 TABLESPOONS EXTRA-VIRGIN OLIVE OIL

1 MEDIUM-SIZE ONION, CHOPPED FINELY

1½ CUPS COOKED WHITE RICE, AT ROOM TEMPERATURE

2 TEASPOONS WHITE TRUFFLE OIL

1 CUP SHREDDED VEGAN AMERICAN OR JACK CHEESE (PAGE 45 OR 42, RESPECTIVELY, OR STORE-BOUGHT)

3 TABLESPOONS CHOPPED FRESH PARSLEY LEAVES

White truffle oil instantly adds an air of sophistication to these stuffed mushrooms, taking them from ordinary to over-the-top awesome. The rice filling can be made a day ahead and refrigerated to eliminate that last minute dash. Then, simply stuff the mushrooms and bake them just before serving.

Preheat the oven to 400°F. Lightly oil a shallow baking pan.

Pull the stems from the mushroom caps. Finely chop the stems and set them aside. Season the mushroom caps with salt and white pepper and place them, rounded side up, in the prepared baking pan. Bake until the mushrooms are tender and starting to release their liquid, about 10 minutes. Remove them from the oven.

Meanwhile, in a skillet, melt the olive oil over medium-high heat for a minute or two, until it slides easily across the skillet. Add the mushroom stems and sauté, stirring, until golden, about 5 minutes. Add the onion, salt, and white pepper to taste and sauté, stirring occasionally, until the onion is golden, about 5 minutes more. In a large bowl, stir the mushroom mixture into the cooked rice, along with the truffle oil and American cheese. Season with more salt and white pepper to taste.

Turn the mushroom caps over and spoon the rice filling into the mushroom caps, pressing gently. There may be filling left over. Bake until the mushrooms are tender, about 20 minutes. Remove from the oven and let cool for 5 minutes, then arrange on a tray and serve hot, sprinkled with the chopped parsley.

yields 20 HORS D'OEUVRES

cheddar chips

This chip and Cheddar combo is a simple and more wholesome home-made version of all those processed nacho cheese chips. Sans the Cheddar, these chips can also fly solo with the other dips in this chapter or as part of the Artisanal Vegan Cheese Platters in Chapter 10.

Preheat the oven to 350°F and place a rack in the upper middle half of the oven. Slice the stack of tortillas crosswise into eight wedges and arrange them on a foil-lined baking sheet.

Place the canola oil and lime juice in a spray-pump mister, and shake well. Spray the tortilla wedges until well moistened.

In a small bowl, stir together the cumin, coriander, chili powder, and salt. Sprinkle over the chips.

Bake the chips for 8 minutes. Rotate the pan and bake watchfully for another 8 minutes, or until the chips are crisp but not browned. Let cool for a few minutes, then serve spread with the Cheddar cheese and your favorite salsa or guacamole.

yields 6 SERVINGS

1 (12-OUNCE) PACKAGE VEGAN SOFT CORN TORTILLAS

1 TABLESPOON CANOLA OIL

3 TABLESPOONS FRESHLY SQUEEZED LIME JUICE, FROM 1 TO 2 LIMES

½ TEASPOON GROUND CUMIN

½ TEASPOON GROUND CORIANDER

1 TEASPOON CHILI POWDER

1 TEASPOON SALT, OR TO TASTE

1 CUP GRATED AND MELTED VEGAN CHEDDAR CHEESE (PAGE 28, OR STORE-BOUGHT)

parmesan popcorn

3 TABLESPOONS COCONUT OIL

½ CUP ORGANIC POPCORN

2 TABLESPOONS VEGAN MARGARINE
(OPTIONAL, IF YOU LIKE DRY POPCORN)

SALT

1 TO 3 TABLESPOONS VEGAN PARMESAN
CHEESE (PAGE 39, OR STORE-BOUGHT)
OR NUTRITIONAL YEAST, OR TO TASTE

Add a hefty dose of cheesiness to your next family movie night by making a few buckets of this quick and easy Parmesan popcorn.

Place the coconut oil in a 6-quart pot over medium heat. Once the oil slides easily across the floor of the pan, place four kernels of popcorn into the pot and cover. Listen for four pops, then remove the pot from the burner, add the remaining popcorn, cover quickly, and let the pot rest for 30 seconds, shaking every 10 seconds to coat the corn, then return the pot to the burner, tightly covered.

Shaking the pot every 20 seconds, listen for the corn to begin popping. When the popping has slowed to 3 seconds between each popping sound, remove the pot from the heat. After about 1 minute, pour the popcorn into a large bowl. Heat the margarine (if using) in the hot pot until it melts, then pour it over the popcorn, sprinkle with the salt and Parmesan cheese, and toss well. Serve promptly.

yields 3 TO 4 AMPLE SERVINGS

swiss mangoes

Tropical mangoes marry well with mellow Swiss cheese in this simple yet captivating appetizer, which also makes a nice and light lunch course or tapas. Just be sure to bring everything to room temperature before serving, for the best flavor.

Plate the Swiss cheese slices, surrounded by the mango slices. Squeeze the lemon wedges over the mango slices to keep them from browning. Serve promptly with the wheat crackers.

yields 6 APPETIZER SERVINGS

20 (¼-INCH) SLICES VEGAN SWISS CHEESE (PAGE 34, OR STORE-BOUGHT)

2 TO 3 MANGOES, PEELED, PITTED, AND SLICED AT THE LAST MINUTE

2 TO 3 LEMON WEDGES

WHEAT CRACKERS

CHAPTER 7

Suppers

Today, everyone's schedule is a crazy-busy nonstop blur of work, school, meetings, practices, housework, homework, and racing from one commitment to another. But one place still offers a safe, quiet island for everyone to gather and escape to once a day, or at least once a week: the supper table. And what's that table without an ooey-gooey icon to hold everything together? If nothing else, this chapter proves that some things, like supper with family and friends, never go out of style.

In this chapter, such dishes as Tomato Gratin with Cheddar Crumbs & Basil Chiffonade, Hot Chili Bean Casserole, My Friend Alfredo, Angel Hair Pasta with Ricotta & Herb Sauce, Baked Cauliflower-Parmesan Penne, Super Fab Fettuccine with Horseradish Cheese Sauce, and Brie & Tomato Pasta Shells stake new claim to the sacredness of the family meal. Their simple prep and rich layers of cheese and other favorite flavors set the stage for relishing and reconnecting with loved ones.

For a more laid-back supper, say for a family movie or game night, turn the cell phones and computers off and maybe even head for the backyard, and let the magic of the All You Can Eat Pizza Buffet do the rest of the work. Mozzarella and Parmesan star in When the Moon Hits Your Eye Cheesy Pizza Pie; Jack and Cheddar help bring it on in Tex-Mex Tortilla Pizza; and hot sauce, Tabasco sauce, and liquid smoke put any meal over the top with Flying Buffalo Pizza.

Finally, never ever forget that the ultimate garnish for any supper dish is good, old-fashioned laughter!

tomato gratin with cheddar crumbs & basil chiffonade

1 (28-OUNCE) CAN ORGANIC DICED TOMATOES, SUCH AS MUIR GLEN, WELL DRAINED

4 CLOVES GARLIC, MINCED IN MINI-PROCESSOR

3 TABLESPOONS CHOPPED FRESH CHIVES OR MINCED GREEN ONIONS (USE A MINI-PROCESSOR)

2 TABLESPOONS DRY MARSALA OR MADEIRA

SALT AND FRESHLY GROUND BLACK PEPPER

1 CUP FRESH VEGAN BREAD CRUMBS, PREFERABLY FRENCH

2 TABLESPOONS PANKO (OPTIONAL)

1½ CUPS GRATED VEGAN CHEDDAR CHEESE (PAGE 28, OR STORE-BOUGHT)

2 TABLESPOONS EXTRA-VIRGIN OLIVE OIL

12 BASIL LEAVES, CUT CHIFFONADE STYLE (SEE PAGE 12)

A convenient year-round baked tomato dish, this could also be served as a side dish at dinner or as a lunch entrée.

Preheat the oven to 350°F. In a large bowl, mix the tomatoes, garlic, 2½ tablespoons of the chives, and Marsala. Season with salt and pepper, and transfer to a 1½-quart gratin or baking dish.

In another large bowl, mix the bread crumbs, panko (if using), Cheddar cheese, and olive oil well. Season with salt and pepper, and sprinkle the mixture over the tomatoes.

Bake until the juices bubble and the topping is golden brown, about 40 minutes. Let stand 10 minutes. Sprinkle with remaining chives and the basil chiffonade, and serve.

yields 2 AMPLE SERVINGS

hot chili bean casserole

1 TABLESPOON CANOLA OIL, FOR
COATING THE SKILLET

1 CUP DICED RED ONION

2 (14-OUNCE) CANS HOT CHILI BEANS,
DRAINED

2 (14-OUNCE) CANS ORGANIC DICED
TOMATOES, SUCH AS MUIR GLEN

1 TEASPOON GARLIC POWDER

1 TEASPOON ONION POWDER

TABASCO SAUCE

1 CUP GRATED VEGAN CHEDDAR OR WINE
CHEESE (PAGE 28 OR 30, RESPECTIVELY,
OR STORE-BOUGHT)

VEGAN SOUR CREAM, FOR SERVING
(PAGE 17, OR STORE-BOUGHT)

Use whatever canned beans you prefer, but I like the extra POW! provided by the hot chili beans (oh yeah, and the sparks of Tabasco!).

Preheat the oven to 400°F. Coat a large nonstick skillet with the canola oil and place it over medium-high heat until hot. Add the onion and sauté until tender, about 8 minutes. Stir in the beans, tomatoes, garlic powder, onion powder, and Tabasco sauce to taste. Cook until heated through completely, stirring often, about 10 minutes.

Transfer the bean mixture into an 8-inch square baking dish. Sprinkle with the Cheddar cheese and bake, uncovered, for 6 to 8 minutes, or until the cheese melts. Let the casserole stand for 5 minutes before serving. Serve with the sour cream.

yields 4 SERVINGS

triple your pleasure fondue

Portraying the flavor and texture of a traditional fondue, this dish takes the heart-warming concept in three new directions of fabulous for the whole family to enjoy. Choose from the Swiss, Smoked Cheddar, or Jack and jalapeño options, or serve all as a tantalizing triad, and let your dippers run wild.

In a large saucepan over medium heat, melt 3 tablespoons of the margarine. Sauté the onion, garlic, and mushrooms, stirring, until the onion has softened, about 5 minutes.

In a medium-size saucepan, combine the soy milk with the onion powder, bouillon cube, flour, celery salt, and soy sauce. Stir over medium heat until the mixture thickens. You may need to add more flour if the mixture doesn't thicken.

Add the mushroom mixture to the soy milk mixture. Puree with an immersion blender, or let cool slightly and process in a standing blender until smooth. Add the cheese of your choice to the mixture, reheat, stir well, and transfer to a fondue pot.

yields 2 SERVINGS

5 TABLESPOONS VEGAN MARGARINE

½ WHITE ONION, MINCED

3 CLOVES GARLIC, PRESSED

2 CUPS TRIMMED AND SLICED WHITE MUSHROOMS

2 CUPS SOY MILK

1 TEASPOON ONION POWDER

1 VEGAN VEGETABLE BOUILLON CUBE

¼ CUP ALL-PURPOSE FLOUR

½ TEASPOON CELERY SALT

1 TABLESPOON VEGAN LOW-SODIUM SOY SAUCE

1½ CUPS (1-INCH-CUBED CUT) VEGAN SWISS, SMOKED CHEDDAR, OR JACK CHEESE WITH FINELY MINCED JALAPEÑOS TO TASTE (OPTIONAL) (PAGE 34, 28, OR 42, RESPECTIVELY, OR STORE-BOUGHT)

suggested dippers

WHOLE MUSHROOMS

BROCCOLI FLORETS

VEGAN FRENCH BREAD CUBES, TOASTED OR NOT

HALVED STEAMED BABY POTATOES

SAUTÉED AND CRISPY BITE-SIZE CUBES OR PIECES OF TOFU OR SEITAN

all you can eat pizza buffet

when the moon hits your eye
cheesy pizza pie

1 (12-INCH) PREPARED VEGAN PIZZA
CRUST

2 TABLESPOONS EXTRA-VIRGIN OLIVE OIL

8 TO 12 OUNCES SHREDDED VEGAN
MOZZARELLA CHEESE (PAGE 31, OR
STORE-BOUGHT)

3 PLUM TOMATOES, PEELED AND DICED

1 TO 2 TABLESPOONS VEGAN PARMESAN
CHEESE (PAGE 39, OR STORE-BOUGHT)

12 FRESH BASIL LEAVES, CUT CHIFFONADE
STYLE (SEE PAGE 12)

1 TEASPOON DRIED OREGANO

RED PEPPER FLAKES (OPTIONAL)

Serve them alone or all together spread across a buffet or picnic table, these three pizzas take everything you ever thought about one of humankind's greatest culinary inventions and add new jolts of sheer delight. Bite by bite, this all-you-can-eat pizza party gives new meaning to quality time!

when the moon hits your eye cheesy pizza pie

Mozzarella and Parmesan cheese conspire to give your pizza night the lift-off it deserves. Also, don't hesitate to add your favorite toppings, including more shredded cheese from Chapter 1, to make this pizza your very own masterpiece. And, to really go the extra mile, start with a fresh batch of Parmesan Garlic Bread (page 101) and serve it with warmed pizza sauce.

Preheat the oven to 450°F. Brush the pizza crust with the olive oil. Scatter the mozzarella cheese and tomatoes over the entire crust. Sprinkle the Parmesan cheese, basil chiffonade, and dried oregano over all. Bake the pizza for 8 to 10 minutes, or until the cheese has melted completely. Sprinkle with the red pepper flakes (if using), let the pizza cool for a few minutes, and then serve.

yields 4 SERVINGS

tex-mex tortilla pizza

You can make this South-of-the-Border pizza nice and spicy by adding chopped jalapeños—or even habaneros—to the toppings. For a Tex-Mex theme meal, start with Amazo-Queso Dip (page 142) and Minced Chipotle Pepper & Cheese Dip (page 149), and then serve the pizza alongside Black Bean & Jalapeño Tacos (page 127).

Preheat the oven to 350°F. In a saucepan over medium heat, heat the refried beans, stirring often. Stir in the seasoning mix.

In a small skillet over medium heat, heat the canola oil. When the oil slides easily across the skillet, carefully place one tortilla in the skillet. After 20 seconds, flip the tortilla and fry it for another 20 seconds. Repeat with the remaining tortillas, draining them on paper towels after they've been cooked.

Arrange the tortillas on a baking sheet. Spread a layer of refried beans on the tortillas, and scatter them generously with the cheese(s) and the corn. Bake the tortillas for 10 to 15 minutes, or until the cheese has melted completely.

Slice the tortillas into wedges and divide them among two to four warmed plates. Garnish the tortilla wedges with the sour cream, tomatoes, green onions, avocado, and black olives. Serve at once.

yields 2 TO 4 SERVINGS

(CONTINUES)

tex-mex tortilla pizza

1 (16-OUNCE) CAN REFRIED BEANS (SEE NOTE)

TACO SEASONING MIX OR CHILI POWDER

1 TABLESPOON CANOLA OIL

4 (6-INCH) VEGAN CORN TORTILLAS

8 OUNCES SHREDDED VEGAN JACK OR CHEDDAR CHEESE, OR A MIXTURE OF BOTH (PAGE 42 OR 28, RESPECTIVELY, OR STORE-BOUGHT)

1/2 TO 3/4 CUP FROZEN CORN KERNELS, THAWED

2 TABLESPOONS VEGAN SOUR CREAM (PAGE 17, OR STORE-BOUGHT)

2 PLUM TOMATOES, PEELED AND DICED

4 GREEN ONIONS, WHITE AND LIGHT GREEN PARTS ONLY, CHOPPED

1 RIPE AVOCADO, PEELED, PITTED, AND DICED

8 PITTED BLACK OLIVES, SLICED

note: Be sure to read the refried beans' can label to make sure they aren't made with lard, as they sometimes are.

flying buffalo pizza

Hot sauce, Tabasco sauce, and liquid smoke make this seitan pizza saucer a round-trip you'll enjoy taking again and again. Also, Flying Buffalo Dip (page 144) and Blue Moon Dip (page 136) are a nice way to launch this sizzling pizza feast.

Preheat the oven to 450°F, placing a rack in the lower third of the oven. In a medium-size bowl, mix the ketchup with the hot sauce, Tabasco sauce, and liquid smoke.

In a medium-size skillet, heat the olive oil over medium heat. Add the onion and cook for 3 to 4 minutes, stirring often. Add the seitan cubes and mushroom quarters, and raise the heat to medium-high. Cook for 4 minutes, or until the mushrooms have softened. Turn off the heat and pour the ketchup mixture into the seitan mixture.

Place the pizza crust on a baking sheet. Spread the seitan mixture over the crust. Top with the cheese(s) of choice and bake for 10 to 15 minutes, until the seitan mixture is bubbling. Top the pizza with the arugula and cucumber, and serve.

yields 2 TO 4 SERVINGS

flying buffalo pizza

1/2 CUP VEGAN KETCHUP

1/4 TO 1/3 CUP FRANK'S RED HOT CAYENNE PEPPER SAUCE

TABASCO SAUCE

1 TEASPOON LIQUID SMOKE

1 TABLESPOON EXTRA-VIRGIN OLIVE OIL

1/2 CUP FINELY CHOPPED YELLOW ONION

8 OUNCES SEITAN, CUT INTO 1/2-INCH CUBES

2 CUPS QUARTERED SHIITAKE MUSHROOM CAPS

1 (12-INCH) PREPARED VEGAN PIZZA CRUST

1 CUP GRATED VEGAN MOZZARELLA CHEESE (PAGE 31, OR STORE-BOUGHT), OR MORE IF NOT USING MUENSTER AND/OR BLUE CHEESE

1 CUP GRATED VEGAN MUENSTER CHEESE (PAGE 44, OR STORE-BOUGHT)

1 CUP CRUMBLY VEGAN BLUE CHEESE (PAGE 41, OR STORE-BOUGHT)

1 CUP WHOLE BABY ARUGULA OR REGULAR ARUGULA, SLICED THINLY

1/2 CUCUMBER, PEELED AND DICED

my friend alfredo

12 OUNCES FIRM TOFU, PRESSED AND
DRAINED (SEE PAGE 18)

1 TEASPOON GARLIC POWDER

1 TEASPOON ONION POWDER

1/2 CUP GRATED VEGAN PARMESAN
CHEESE (PAGE 39, OR STORE-BOUGHT)

1 TABLESPOON CANOLA OIL

4 BASIL LEAVES, TORN ROUGHLY OR
CHOPPED

1/2 TEASPOON FRESHLY GROUND WHITE
PEPPER

1/4 TO 1/3 CUP SOY MILK

1/2 POUND VEGAN NOODLES, COOKED
ACCORDING TO THE MANUFACTURER'S
INSTRUCTIONS AND STIRRED WITH
2 TABLESPOONS OF VEGAN MARGARINE

Meet your new mealtime BFF. Unlike many heavy, dairy-based Alfredos, this one is light and smooth. The flavor combo of garlic and onion powders, Parmesan cheese, basil, and ground white pepper makes sure that this Alfredo warms your heart from the very beginning.

In a blender, combine all the ingredients, except the noodles. Blend until fairly smooth.

Transfer the mixture to a large saucepan and heat to just below boiling over medium heat, stirring.

Serve this luscious sauce over the buttery noodles.

yields 4 SERVINGS

angel hair pasta with ricotta & herb sauce

1 POUND DRIED OR FRESH ANGEL HAIR PASTA (CAPELLINI)

1 CUP VEGAN RICOTTA CHEESE (PAGE 40, OR STORE-BOUGHT)

4 CLOVES GARLIC, ROASTED UNPEELED AND PRESSED INTO THE RICOTTA

2 TEASPOONS MINCED FRESH OREGANO LEAVES

1 TEASPOON MINCED FRESH CILANTRO LEAVES

1 TEASPOON MINCED FRESH MINT LEAVES

1 CUP FROZEN CORN KERNELS, THAWED

This heavenly ricotta cheese and corn pasta dish accented with garlic, oregano, cilantro, and mint would be ideal served on a blustery winter evening but fits the bill anytime you want a soothing dose of *ahhhhh*.

Bring a large pot of salted water to a boil and cook the angel hair pasta according to the manufacturer's instructions.

In a blender, combine the ricotta cheese and roasted garlic, as well as the oregano, cilantro, and mint leaves, and blend until smooth.

Transfer the ricotta mixture to a large saucepan, stir in the corn, and bring to a near simmer over medium heat, stirring frequently.

Drain the pasta and divide it among four warmed individual pasta bowls or plates. Serve ladled with the ricotta cheese sauce to taste.

yields 4 SERVINGS

three-cheese screwy fusilli

"Yum!" has a new name. Accented with a smooth Dijon mustard, parsley, green onions, and white truffle oil, I challenge you to find even a single bite of leftovers when you serve this baked ricotta-Cheddar-Parmesan pasta dish to family and friends.

In a kettle, bring 6 quarts of water to a boil and add 2 tablespoons of salt. Add the fusilli, stir, and cook until not quite al dente, about 10 minutes. Drain thoroughly.

Preheat the oven to 350°F. Meanwhile, in a large bowl, mix the egg replacer with the soy milk, ricotta cheese, mustard, and white truffle oil. Add black pepper to taste, and the parsley, green onions, and 1 teaspoon of salt. Toss the hot fusilli in the sauce, then fold in the Cheddar cheese.

Coat the inside of a large (2½-quart) oval enameled cast-iron gratin dish with olive oil. Spoon the fusilli mixture into the dish. Sprinkle with the Parmesan cheese and panko, and drizzle with the 2 tablespoons of olive oil.

Bake until the top is browned, the fusilli is crisping, and the sauce is bubbling, about 40 minutes.

yields 6 SERVINGS

SALT

1 POUND DRIED FUSILLI, PREFERABLY MULTICOLORED

⅓ CUP VEGAN EGG REPLACER OR FLAXSEED MIXTURE (⅓ CUP FILTERED OR BOTTLED WATER BLENDED WELL WITH 2 TABLESPOONS GROUND FLAXSEEDS)

1½ CUPS SOY MILK

½ CUP VEGAN RICOTTA CHEESE (PAGE 40, OR STORE-BOUGHT)

2 TABLESPOONS SMOOTH VEGAN DIJON MUSTARD

1 TEASPOON WHITE TRUFFLE OIL

FRESHLY GROUND BLACK PEPPER

¼ CUP MINCED FRESH PARSLEY LEAVES

1 CUP MINCED GREEN ONIONS, WITH 1 INCH OF THE GREEN (USE A MINI-PROCESSOR)

3 CUPS GRATED SHARP VEGAN CHEDDAR CHEESE (PAGE 28, OR STORE-BOUGHT)

2 TABLESPOONS EXTRA-VIRGIN OLIVE OIL, PLUS MORE FOR GREASING THE GRATIN DISH

½ CUP FRESHLY GRATED VEGAN PARMESAN CHEESE (PAGE 39, OR STORE-BOUGHT)

½ CUP VEGAN PANKO

four-cheese baked rigatoni gratin

Luxurious and satisfying (and decadent, and scrumptious, and . . . well, you get the point), this gratin boasts a quadruple burst of cheesy pleasure that's relatively easy to make. However, the longer the tomato and vermouth sauce simmers, the better and more soothing.

Preferably in an enameled cast-iron kettle over medium heat, melt the margarine in the peanut oil. Add the carrot, celery, and onion, and stir until the ingredients are well coated with the buttery oil. Cook the mixture until it softens, about 5 minutes, then season with the salt and pepper.

Add the soy milk, lower the heat, and simmer until the milk all but disappears, 20 minutes or so. Pour in the vermouth and let it bubble down for 20 minutes as well.

Add the tomatoes and sun-dried tomatoes, and stir well. Let the sauce simmer very gently for at least 1 hour, and up to 4 hours.

When you're ready to proceed, preheat the oven to 350°F, and rub margarine inside a 14-inch (2½-quart) oval gratin dish, preferably enameled cast iron.

In a large pot, boil the rigatoni in salted water just until al dente, about 7 minutes. Drain the rigatoni well, then return it to its pot and stir in the tomato sauce. Finally, stir in the parsley.

Pour half the rigatoni mixture into the gratin. Roughly spread it with the soft ricotta cheese, and sprinkle with the Swiss cheese and Parmesan cheese. Cover with the remaining pasta. Arrange the mozzarella slices over all.

Bake for about 20 minutes, until bubbly, then run the gratin watchfully under a broiler just until the cheese browns lightly and the pasta begins to crisp on top.

Let the pasta rest for 5 minutes, then serve.

yields 4 VERY EXTRAVAGANT SERVINGS

2 TABLESPOONS VEGAN MARGARINE

2 TABLESPOONS PEANUT OIL

1 CARROT, MINCED

1 CELERY STALK, MINCED

1 MEDIUM-SIZE ONION, MINCED

A GENEROUS PINCH OF SALT

FRESHLY GROUND BLACK PEPPER

1 CUP SOY MILK

½ CUP WHITE VERMOUTH OR DRY WHITE WINE

1 (28-OUNCE) CAN DICED TOMATOES, WITH THEIR JUICE, MUIR GLEN PREFERRED

12 SUN-DRIED TOMATOES, NOT PACKED IN OIL, PREFERABLY UNSALTED, CHOPPED ROUGHLY (SEE NOTE ON PAGE 21)

1 POUND RIGATONI

¼ CUP FRESHLY CHOPPED ITALIAN (FLAT-LEAF) PARSLEY

1 CUP VEGAN RICOTTA CHEESE (PAGE 40, OR STORE-BOUGHT), AT ROOM TEMPERATURE

1½ CUPS GRATED VEGAN SWISS CHEESE (PAGE 34, OR STORE-BOUGHT)

¼ CUP FRESHLY GRATED VEGAN PARMESAN CHEESE (PAGE 39, OR STORE-BOUGHT)

½ POUND VEGAN MOZZARELLA (PAGE 31, OR STORE-BOUGHT), CUT INTO ½-INCH SLICES

baked cauliflower-parmesan penne

1/4 CUP FRESH, SLIGHTLY COARSE
VEGAN BREAD CRUMBS

1/4 CUP VEGAN PANKO

1 SMALL HEAD CAULIFLOWER, OR 1/2
LARGE HEAD, CUT INTO 3/4-INCH FLORETS

2 TABLESPOONS EXTRA-VIRGIN OLIVE OIL

SALT AND FRESHLY GROUND BLACK
PEPPER

1 CLOVE GARLIC, MINCED OR PRESSED

3 GREEN ONIONS, WHITE PARTS CHOPPED
FINELY, GREEN PARTS CUT INTO 1/2-INCH
PIECES

TABASCO SAUCE OR RED PEPPER FLAKES

8 OUNCES GEMELLI OR MULTICOLORED
FUSILLI

1/3 CUP PINE NUTS, TOASTED LIGHTLY
(SEE INSTRUCTIONS ON PAGE 30)

1/2 CUP PITTED AND COARSELY CHOPPED
KALAMATA OLIVES

1/4 CUP VEGAN PARMESAN CHEESE
(PAGE 39, OR STORE-BOUGHT)

Roasting cauliflower brings out a lovely sweetness in this vastly underappreciated vegetable that counterpoints the lusty background flavor of the olives in the sauce.

Preheat the oven to 450°F. In a large pot, bring 6 to 8 quarts of water to a boil. On a foil-lined jelly-roll pan, toss the bread crumbs with the panko, and watchfully toast the mixture in the middle of the oven until golden brown, 3 to 4 minutes. Transfer to a bowl and set aside.

Toss the cauliflower with the olive oil right on the jelly-roll pan and season with the salt and pepper. Roast in the middle of the oven, stirring occasionally, until the cauliflower is tender and begins to brown, about 15 minutes. Set aside. Lower the oven heat to 325°F.

In a large skillet over medium heat, sauté the garlic and green onion whites until soft, about 4 minutes. Add Tabasco sauce to taste and cook for another minute or two.

Remove the skillet from the heat while you cook the pasta according to the package directions. Just before the pasta is al dente, 10 to 11 minutes, add the cauliflower, pine nuts, and half the toasted bread crumbs to the skillet. Toss the mixture well.

When the pasta is ready, reserve a cup of its cooking water, drain the pasta, and add it to the skillet with 1/2 cup (more or less) of the cooking water. Stir in the olives and green onion greens. Transfer the pasta mixture to a 2 1/2-quart gratin or baking dish and bake in the middle of the oven until the pasta on top begins to crisp, 8 to 10 minutes. Drizzle with the remaining olive oil to refresh the pasta, and sprinkle it with the rest of the crumbs and the Parmesan cheese. Serve warm.

yields 2 QUITE AMPLE SERVINGS

lemony parmesan linguine

Lemon marries so happily with pasta, and the Parmesan cheese really deepens the complex flavors in this refreshing go-to linguine dish.

In a small skillet over medium heat, melt the margarine and stir in the bread crumbs. Stir until toasted. Set aside.

Bring a large pot of salted water to a boil. In a bowl, with a fork, blend the egg replacer with the soy milk, Parmesan cheese, lemon zest and juice, salt, and pepper. Taste the sauce and if you want it more lemony, add more juice.

When the pasta is just al dente, remove and reserve about 1 cup of the cooking liquid, drain the pasta, and return it to the pot. Toss in the remaining 4 tablespoons of margarine and stir and swirl until all the pasta is coated.

Stir in the egg replacer mixture and turn the pasta in it, adding a few tablespoons of the cooking liquid if it looks a bit dry.

Place in serving bowls and sprinkle with parsley and the buttered bread crumbs.

yields 4 SERVINGS

2 TABLESPOONS VEGAN MARGARINE, PLUS 4 TABLESPOONS (1/2 STICK) FOR TOSSING THE PASTA

1/2 CUP DRIED VEGAN BREAD CRUMBS

1/3 CUP VEGAN EGG REPLACER

1/2 CUP SOY MILK

1/2 CUP GRATED VEGAN PARMESAN CHEESE (PAGE 39, OR STORE-BOUGHT)

ZEST OF 1 LEMON AND JUICE OF 1/2 LEMON, PLUS MORE JUICE, IF DESIRED

1 TEASPOON SALT

FRESHLY GROUND WHITE PEPPER

1 POUND LINGUINE

2 TABLESPOONS MINCED FRESH PARSLEY

super fab fettuccine with horseradish cheese sauce

1 POUND DRIED FETTUCCINE

2 TABLESPOONS VEGAN MARGARINE

2 TABLESPOONS ALL-PURPOSE FLOUR

1 CUP SOY MILK

2 CLOVES GARLIC, PRESSED

1 CUP SHREDDED VEGAN CHEDDAR
OR HORSERADISH CHEDDAR CHEESE
(PAGE 28, OR STORE-BOUGHT)

1 TABLESPOON VEGAN PREPARED WHITE
HORSERADISH

SALT AND FRESHLY GROUND BLACK
PEPPER

This is a mighty zip-zip-zippy pasta dish. And for all my fellow eccentrics out there, you can make it even zippier by grating in some fresh peeled horseradish or going for the Horseradish Cheddar cheese option.

Bring a large pot of salted water to a boil. Cook the fettuccine according to the manufacturer's directions. Drain the cooked fettuccine and return to the pot.

Meanwhile, in a medium-size skillet, melt the margarine. Add the flour and cook, stirring, for 3 minutes. Pour in the soy milk and add the garlic. When the milk mixture comes to a simmer, add the Cheddar cheese, a handful at a time, stirring constantly. When the cheese has melted, remove the skillet from the heat and stir in the horseradish and salt and pepper to taste.

Pour the sauce over the fettuccine in the pot and toss until well mixed. Serve at once.

yields 4 SERVINGS

chedda-peppa pasta

With a name worthy of a foodie Rap duo, Cheddar cheese busts a move with everyday spaghetti in this effortlessly smooth and creamy pasta dish, all accented with balsamic vinegar.

Bring a large pot of salted water to a boil. Add the spaghetti and cook according to the manufacturer's instructions, until al dente. Drain the spaghetti, reserving 2 cups of the cooking water.

Return the pasta and cooking water to the pot and place over low heat. Add the Cheddar cheese, olive oil, and pepper, and stir until the cheese and olive oil have melted into a creamy sauce, about 5 minutes. Season with salt to taste and serve, offering additional Cheddar cheese and balsamic vinegar at the table.

yields 4 SERVINGS

1 POUND SPAGHETTI OR BUCATINI

2 CUPS SHREDDED VEGAN CHEDDAR OR WINE CHEESE (PAGE 28 OR 30, RESPECTIVELY, OR STORE-BOUGHT) (ABOUT 5 OUNCES), PLUS MORE FOR SERVING

3 TABLESPOONS EXTRA-VIRGIN OLIVE OIL

1 TO 2 TEASPOONS COARSELY GROUND BLACK PEPPERCORNS

SALT

BALSAMIC VINEGAR, FOR SERVING

brie & tomato pasta shells

4 RIPE LARGE TOMATOES, CUT INTO
$\frac{1}{2}$-INCH CUBES, OR 1 (28-OUNCE) CAN
DICED ORGANIC TOMATOES, DRAINED

2 CUPS ($\frac{1}{3}$-INCH-CUBED) VEGAN BRIE
CHEESE (PAGE 33, OR STORE-BOUGHT)

2 TEASPOONS MINCED FRESH THYME
LEAVES

1 TEASPOON MINCED FRESH OREGANO
LEAVES

3 CLOVES GARLIC, PRESSED

1 CUP EXTRA-VIRGIN OLIVE OIL

2 TEASPOONS SALT

$\frac{1}{2}$ TEASPOON FRESHLY GROUND
BLACK PEPPER

1 POUND LARGE PASTA SHELLS

When you want to impress all those cheese snobs around the dinner table, present them with this simple and elegant Brie dish that will literally leave them speechless.

At least 2 hours before serving, in a large individual pasta bowl, combine the tomatoes, Brie cheese, thyme, oregano, garlic, olive oil, salt, and pepper. Set aside, covered, and let rest at room temperature for 2 or more hours.

In a large saucepan, bring an ample amount of salted water to a boil. Add the pasta shells and boil until the shells are al dente, 8 to 10 minutes.

Drain the shells and immediately toss with the tomato sauce. Serve promptly.

yields 4 SERVINGS

CHAPTER 8

Mac 'n' Cheese

Let's see: So decadent it should be outlawed, scrumptious beyond belief, salaciously delish, uncompromisingly yummy. And historical!

Its European forbearers date back hundreds of years and include what's believed to be the first recorded cheesy mac recipe from a 1769 cookbook, *The Experienced English Housekeeper* by Elizabeth Raffald. But President Thomas Jefferson is credited with making macaroni and cheese as American as apple pie from the time he first served a version of it at a state dinner in 1802.

My friends, no Second Coming of cheese would be complete without the following all-star incarnations of the ultimate rock-my-world comfort food known simply as mac 'n' cheese.

In this case, you can believe the hype about performances by the likes of Two-Cheese Macaroni with Caramelized Shallots; Creamy Seasoned Macaroni; Parmesan-Cheddar-Swiss Skillet Macaroni; Mac 'n' Cheese with Ground Cashews & Truffle Oil; Mac & Jack; and Spicy Hot Mac Attack!

Served to a family night table full of picky eaters, a gathering of discerning friends, or while cuddled up on the couch, these mac 'n' cheese recipes will satisfy, satisfy, satisfy your craving for the good life, one messy bite at a time. Also, consider preparing several of them for an unforgettable buffet theme at your next party.

BTW, I can confirm the longstanding rumors that these dishes just happen to be a remedy for mood swings, bad hair days, breakups, stressful situations, run-ins with cranky bosses, temperamental teens, negative energy, traffic jams… and I would never underestimate the power of mac 'n' cheese in helping to facilitate world peace.

In fact, if good karma has a signature lineup of dishes, you're looking at them!

creamy seasoned macaroni

Mealtime doesn't get any cozier than when cream cheese, Cheddar cheese, mustard, grated nutmeg, and white truffle oil revamp this elegantly seasoned, vegan variation on a classic dish.

Preheat the oven to 375°F and position a rack in the upper third of the oven. Use 1 tablespoon of the margarine to grease a 9-inch glass round or square baking pan, or use a 2½-quart enameled cast-iron gratin dish, especially if you want a nice dark crust to form at the bottom of the macaroni and cheese.

In a large bowl, combine the cream cheese, soy milk, mustard, cayenne pepper, nutmeg, salt, and pepper. Puree the mixture with an immersion blender (or combine the ingredients in a standing blender and puree them).

Reserve about ¼ cup of the Cheddar cheese for topping, and stir the remaining 1¾ cups of cheese into the milk mixture. Stir in the uncooked elbow macaroni. Pour the mixture into the greased pan, cover tightly with foil, and bake for 30 minutes.

Uncover the pan, stir gently, sprinkle with the reserved cheese, and dot with the remaining tablespoon of margarine. Bake, uncovered, for 25 to 30 minutes longer, until browned and bubbling. Let cool at least 10 minutes before serving. Drizzle with the white truffle oil to serve, if desired.

yields 2 TO 4 SERVINGS

2 TABLESPOONS VEGAN MARGARINE

1 CUP VEGAN CREAM CHEESE OR COTTAGE CHEESE (PAGE 37 OR 36, RESPECTIVELY, OR STORE-BOUGHT)

2 CUPS SOY MILK

2 TEASPOONS DRY MUSTARD, SUCH AS COLMAN'S

PINCH OF CAYENNE PEPPER

PINCH OF FRESHLY GRATED NUTMEG

½ TEASPOON SALT

¼ TEASPOON FRESHLY GROUND WHITE PEPPER, OR MORE TO TASTE

2 CUPS GRATED VEGAN SHARP CHEDDAR CHEESE (PAGE 28, OR STORE-BOUGHT)

½ POUND ELBOW MACARONI

WHITE TRUFFLE OIL, FOR SERVING (OPTIONAL)

parmesan-cheddar-swiss skillet macaroni

1 POUND SHORT PASTA, SUCH AS SHELLS, PENNE, OR FARFALLE (BOW-TIE)

KOSHER SALT

4 TABLESPOONS (½ STICK) VEGAN MARGARINE, PLUS 1 TO 2 TABLESPOONS FOR TOPPING

¼ CUP UNBLEACHED ALL-PURPOSE FLOUR

3 CUPS SOY MILK

1 TEASPOON DRY MUSTARD, PREFERABLY COLMAN'S, OR TO TASTE

TABASCO SAUCE

1 CUP GRATED VEGAN PARMESAN CHEESE (PAGE 39, OR STORE-BOUGHT), PLUS ½ CUP FOR TOPPING

2 CUPS GRATED SHARP VEGAN CHEDDAR CHEESE (PAGE 28, OR STORE-BOUGHT)

1 CUP GRATED VEGAN SWISS CHEESE (PAGE 34, OR STORE-BOUGHT)

2 TABLESPOONS CHOPPED FRESH THYME, ROSEMARY, AND/OR SAGE

2 CUPS COARSE FRESH VEGAN BREAD CRUMBS

The fresh herbs in this everyday macaroni and three-cheese spectacular really come through, but you can always add more to taste. Also, using a cast-iron skillet will ensure a crunchy bottom crust.

Preheat the oven to 400°F. Bring a pot of salted water to a boil and cook the pasta until nearly al dente but not fully cooked. Drain it and rinse lightly with cool water.

In an 11-inch cast-iron or nonstick skillet, melt the 4 tablespoons of margarine until the foam subsides, then add the flour, whisking to prevent burning. Add the soy milk slowly, whisking constantly. Whisk in the dry mustard, Tabasco sauce, and teaspoon of kosher salt.

Add the 1 cup of Parmesan cheese, and the Cheddar and Swiss cheeses a little at a time, stirring often, until they melt into the sauce. Taste for salt and spiciness, and adjust as needed.

Turn off the heat and add the drained pasta little by little, stirring to coat with the sauce. In a small bowl, combine the herbs, bread crumbs, and the remaining ½ cup of Parmesan cheese, and sprinkle over the top. Crumble the remaining margarine into small pieces over the whole skillet.

Bake until the top is browned and the sauce is bubbling, 20 to 25 minutes. Let the macaroni and cheese rest for 5 minutes before serving.

yields 4 AMPLE SERVINGS

mac 'n' cheese with ground cashews & truffle oil

Even if served on the most ordinary of days, this macaroni dish with several cheese options has special occasion written all over it . . . and with white and black truffles to boot.

In a food processor, pulse the bread until you've made crumbs. Set the crumbs aside and wipe out the processor. Then, mince, in this order: garlic, shallots, celery, and mushrooms, pulsing the latter three vegetables just until nicely chopped.

In a heavy, large, stainless-steel skillet over medium heat, melt the margarine. Add the processed ingredients and sauté until tender, stirring, about 6 minutes. Add the vermouth (or dry white wine) and simmer until almost all the liquid has evaporated, about 10 minutes.

Add the soy milk, miso paste, thyme, and bay leaf to the skillet, and bring just to a simmer. Reduce the mixture over low heat for about 15 minutes, then remove the skillet from the heat. Add the Cheddar cheese and stir until melted and smooth. Sprinkle with the Parmesan cheese. Remove the bay leaf and puree the mixture with an immersion blender (or carefully, in batches, in a standing blender, and return to the same skillet). Stir in the black truffle (if using). Season with salt and white pepper.

Heat the broiler. In a large pot of boiling salted water, cook the macaroni until just tender but still firm to the bite. Drain very well.

While the pasta is cooking, make the crumb topping by combining the topping ingredients.

Then, in a small bowl, mix the bread crumbs set aside in the beginning, green onions, parsley, and ground cashews. In a medium-size skillet over medium heat, melt the margarine. Add the bread crumb mixture and sauté, stirring, until golden and coated with margarine, about 2 minutes.

Add the cooked pasta to the sauce in the skillet, then stir in the white truffle oil (or 1/2 teaspoon white truffle powder). Toss to coat. Pour into a large gratin dish and top with the crumb topping. Broil watchfully until the topping is crisp and golden brown, 2 to 3 minutes. Serve at once.

yields 4 SERVINGS

ENOUGH CRUSTLESS VEGAN BREAD TO MAKE 1 CUP OF CRUMBS

1 CLOVE GARLIC, PEELED

2 SHALLOTS, PEELED

1 CELERY STALK, TRIMMED AND CHOPPED

6 MEDIUM-SIZE BUTTON MUSHROOMS, SLICED

2 TABLESPOONS VEGAN MARGARINE, PLUS MORE FOR A SECOND ROUND OF SAUTÉING

1 1/2 CUPS DRY WHITE VERMOUTH

3 CUPS SOY MILK

1/4 CUP MISO PASTE

1 TEASPOON FRESH THYME LEAVES

1 BAY LEAF

2 CUPS GRATED VEGAN CHEDDAR, SWISS, OR JACK CHEESE (PAGE 28, 34, OR 42, RESPECTIVELY, OR STORE-BOUGHT)

1/4 CUP VEGAN PARMESAN CHEESE (PAGE 39, OR STORE-BOUGHT)

1 TABLESPOON CHOPPED WHOLE BLACK TRUFFLE FROM A GLASS JAR, OR WHOLE DRIED BLACK TRUFFLE (OPTIONAL)

SALT AND FRESHLY GROUND WHITE PEPPER

1 POUND ELBOW MACARONI

1/4 CUP CHOPPED GREEN ONIONS

1/4 CUP CHOPPED FRESH PARSLEY

1/2 CUP FINELY GROUND CASHEWS

1 TEASPOON WHITE TRUFFLE OIL

crumb topping

1 CUP FRESH VEGAN BREAD CRUMBS

2 TABLESPOONS MINCED GREEN ONIONS (USE A MINI-PROCESSOR)

2 TABLESPOONS VEGAN MARGARINE

mac & jack

½ POUND ELBOW MACARONI

4 TABLESPOONS (½ STICK) VEGAN
MARGARINE, CUT INTO BITS,
OR CANOLA OIL

TABASCO SAUCE

¾ CUP SOY MILK, POSSIBLY MORE,
IF NEEDED

¼ CUP VEGAN EGG REPLACER

1 TEASPOON DRY MUSTARD, SUCH AS
COLMAN'S, DISSOLVED IN A LITTLE WATER

2 CUPS GRATED VEGAN JACK CHEESE
(PAGE 42, OR STORE-BOUGHT)

SALT AND FRESHLY GROUND WHITE
PEPPER

Be prepared to whip up this bowl of bliss morning, noon, and night to get your cheesy mac quick fix. With a little help from Jack cheese, the Tabasco sauce and dry mustard give the elbow macaroni a distinctive edge.

Preheat the oven to 350°F. Boil the macaroni in plenty of salted water until just barely done, 6 to 8 minutes. Drain the pasta and toss with the margarine in a large, ovenproof mixing bowl.

In a small bowl, mix the Tabasco sauce to taste into the soy milk. Reserving about ⅓ cup, stir the mixture into the macaroni, then add the egg replacer, mustard, and three-quarters of the Jack cheese. When well combined, season to taste with salt and pepper, and set the bowl directly in the oven.

Every 5 minutes, remove the bowl briefly to stir in some of the reserved cheese, adding more soy milk as necessary to keep the mixture moist. When all the cheese has been incorporated and the mixture is hot and creamy (which should take 20 minutes, in all), serve it at once, with a plate of vegan crackers to crumble over.

yields 4 SERVINGS

whole-grain macaroni with cottage cheese & cheddar

The comparatively chewy texture of the whole-grain macaroni stands up well to the gooey Cheddar cheese, while the cottage cheese brings it all together in this harmonious family-style feast.

Preheat the oven to 350°F. Generously grease a 2½-quart baking dish with the canola oil. In a large bowl, combine the cottage cheese, sour cream, salt, garlic powder, onion powder, and white pepper. Add the Cheddar cheese and toss until well mixed. Stir in the cooked macaroni.

Transfer the mixture to the prepared baking dish and bake, uncovered, for 30 minutes or until heated through and bubbly. Sprinkle with the paprika and serve.

yields 4 TO 6 SERVINGS

CANOLA OIL, FOR GREASING THE BAKING DISH

2 CUPS VEGAN COTTAGE CHEESE (PAGE 36, OR STORE-BOUGHT)

8 OUNCES VEGAN SOUR CREAM (PAGE 17, OR STORE-BOUGHT)

¾ TEASPOON SALT

½ TEASPOON GARLIC POWDER

½ TEASPOON ONION POWDER

1 TEASPOON FRESHLY GROUND WHITE PEPPER

2 CUPS SHREDDED VEGAN CHEDDAR CHEESE, THE SHARPER THE BETTER (PAGE 28, OR STORE-BOUGHT)

½ POUND WHOLE-GRAIN ELBOW MACARONI, COOKED ACCORDING TO THE MANUFACTURER'S INSTRUCTIONS AND WELL DRAINED

½ TO 1 TEASPOON SMOKED SPANISH PAPRIKA

two-cheese macaroni with caramelized shallots

3 TABLESPOONS CANOLA OIL, PLUS
MORE FOR GREASING THE GRATIN DISH

3 CUPS SLICED SHALLOTS (ABOUT
6 LARGE SHALLOTS)

KOSHER SALT AND FRESHLY GROUND
WHITE PEPPER

½ POUND ELBOW MACARONI

1¼ CUPS SOY MILK

2 TEASPOONS TABASCO SAUCE,
OR MORE TO TASTE

2 CUPS COARSELY GRATED VEGAN
CHEDDAR CHEESE (ABOUT 8 OUNCES)
(PAGE 28, OR STORE-BOUGHT)

1½ TABLESPOONS ALL-PURPOSE FLOUR

⅔ CUP CRUMBLED VEGAN FETA CHEESE
(PAGE 35, OR STORE-BOUGHT)

note: *Vegan feta cheese can be pretty salty. If you want to avoid that, swap it out for vegan ricotta (page 40, or store-bought).*

Cheddar and feta cheese work with Tabasco sauce and caramelized onions to transform elbow macaroni from wallflower into the life of the party anytime you want!

Preheat the oven to 400°F. Rub a 1½-quart (smallish) gratin dish with canola oil. In a heavy, large skillet over medium-high heat, melt the 3 tablespoons of canola oil. Add the shallots and sprinkle them with salt and white pepper. Cover the skillet and cook for 5 minutes, stirring often. Lower the heat to medium. Cook, covered, until the shallots are deep brown, stirring often, 6 to 8 minutes.

Meanwhile, in a large saucepan of boiling water, cook the macaroni until just tender, but still firm to the bite, 6 to 7 minutes, stirring occasionally. Drain well and reserve the saucepan.

In the reserved saucepan over medium heat, bring the soy milk and Tabasco sauce to a simmer. In a medium-size bowl, toss the Cheddar cheese with the flour to coat, then add the mixture to the soy milk. Whisk until the mixture is smooth and just returns to a simmer, about 2 minutes. Stir in the al dente macaroni and season with salt and white pepper.

Spread the macaroni mixture in the prepared gratin dish. Top with the shallots, then the feta cheese. Sprinkle with white pepper. Bake until heated through, about 15 minutes.

yields 4 TO 6 SERVINGS

spicy hot mac attack!

Sautéed and softened hot chile peppers give this beaut a liveliness that'll leave you defenseless in the luscious wake of Cheddar cheese, garlic, thyme, rosemary, and more. Obviously, you should temper the spiciness according to your and your guests' tastes by holding back or increasing (!!!) the number of peppers you use.

Preheat the oven to 350°F. Grease a 2½-quart baking dish with the canola oil.

In a roomy saucepan over medium heat, melt the margarine. Add the flour and cook, stirring, until bubbly. Add the soy milk, cream cheese, garlic, thyme, rosemary, and 1 teaspoon of white pepper. Cook, stirring constantly, until the mixture has thickened.

Add the Cheddar cheese and hot peppers (if using). Stir until the cheese has melted. Add salt and additional pepper to taste.

Combine the sauce with the pasta and stir well. Spoon into the prepared baking dish and bake until bubbly, about 25 minutes. To brown the top of the dish, watchfully run it under a hot broiler for a few minutes.

yields 4 SERVINGS

CANOLA OIL, FOR GREASING THE BAKING DISH

4 TABLESPOONS (½ STICK) VEGAN MARGARINE

3 TABLESPOONS ALL-PURPOSE FLOUR

1½ CUPS SOY MILK

8 OUNCES VEGAN CREAM CHEESE, SOFTENED (PAGE 37, OR STORE-BOUGHT)

2 CLOVES GARLIC, PRESSED

1 TEASPOON MINCED FRESH THYME LEAVES

1 TEASPOON MINCED FRESH ROSEMARY LEAVES

1 TEASPOON FRESHLY GROUND WHITE PEPPER, PLUS MORE AS NEEDED

8 OUNCES GRATED VEGAN CHEDDAR CHEESE (PAGE 28, OR STORE-BOUGHT)

2 TO 4 JALAPEÑOS, STEMMED, SEEDED, AND MINCED (OPTIONAL)

1 TO 2 HABANERO PEPPERS, STEMMED, SEEDED, AND MINCED (OPTIONAL)

SALT

½ POUND ELBOW MACARONI, COOKED ACCORDING TO THE MANUFACTURER'S INSTRUCTIONS AND WELL DRAINED

CHAPTER 9

Cheesecake

A favorite for family night dinners, friendly get-togethers, birthday parties, anniversary celebrations, wedding and baby showers, backyard barbecues, guys' and ladies' nights out, a quiet night at home on the couch (watching a *Golden Girls* marathon!), and even for satisfying Olympic-size cravings.

Ancient Greeks first discovered the Fountain of Delicious known as cheesecake four thousand years ago, with evidence suggesting it was even served to athletes competing in the first Olympic games in 776 BC. The first recorded cheesecake recipe was written by ancient foodie Athenaeus in AD 230, and now, a few centuries later, the vegan homages that follow contribute a new chapter to this illustrious history.

When you finish off any occasion with the Vanilla, Strawberry, Chocolate, Blueberry, and Banana Cheesecake Extravaganza, Pecan-Crusted Cheesecake Bars, White Chocolate Cheesecake Petit Fours, or Cheesecake Party Parfaits, you are loudly and clearly saying, "I LOVE YOU!" to yourself and your guests with every single bite.

Because these recipes have several ingredients in common, including the homemade vegan cream cheese (page 37), consult "The Cheesy Vegan Pantry" for more information on vegan graham crackers (page 11), vegan chocolate (page 7), and berries (page 7).

I'm a firm believer that because our lives are so crazy-busy, it's important to treat ourselves to something every single day. The cheesecake recipes on the following pages are treats of the highest order. They are gifts that keep on giving time and again, both to us as home cooks and to the loved ones we are serving.

Also, they definitely prove that the way to a person's heart is through his or her sweet tooth.

the cheesecake extravaganza

1 TABLESPOON VEGAN MARGARINE, MELTED

3 TABLESPOONS VEGAN GRAHAM CRACKER CRUMBS

1 (14-OUNCE) PACKAGE EXTRA-FIRM SILKEN TOFU, PRESSED AND DRAINED (SEE PAGE 18)

1 CUP VEGAN CREAM CHEESE, SOFTENED (PAGE 37, OR STORE-BOUGHT)

¼ CUP VEGAN EGG REPLACER

½ CUP VEGAN SUGAR, PLUS 2 TABLESPOONS FOR OPTIONAL SWIRLED TOPPING

2 TEASPOONS VANILLA EXTRACT

4 TO 6 OUNCES FRESH STRAWBERRIES OR BLUEBERRIES, FOR OPTIONAL SWIRLED TOPPING

TOPPINGS OF CHOICE (OPTIONAL)

This stand-alone vanilla cheesecake recipe also lends itself to an eye-popping quartet of strawberry, chocolate, blueberry, and banana adaptations (see page 211). Serve each alone or surprise family and friends with a lineup of two or more of these cheesecakes for an unforgettable dessert extravaganza. Just remember one thing before all caution goes out the door with the first forkful: resist the overwhelming temptation to devour this cheesecake before it has been refrigerated for at least four hours.

Preheat the oven to 350°F. Brush the sides and bottom of a 9-inch springform pan or glass pie plate with the margarine. Sprinkle the graham cracker crumbs over the bottom of the pan and tilt it to coat it evenly with the crumbs.

In a food processor or standing mixer, blend the tofu, cream cheese, egg replacer, ½ cup of sugar, and vanilla until smooth. Pour the tofu mixture into the piecrust.

For optional strawberry or blueberry swirl: Before baking the cheesecake, in a food processor, puree the berries, strain through a fine-mesh strainer, and discard any leftover pieces of the berries. Add 2 tablespoons of vegan sugar to the puree, whisking until well blended. Drop teaspoon or so size dollops of the puree on top of the cheesecake, then using a knife or toothpick, swirl the berry puree as desired.

Bake the cheesecake for about 30 minutes.

Turn off the oven, and allow the cheesecake to sit in the oven for another 40 minutes. Remove the cheesecake from the oven and allow it to cool. Refrigerate for at least 4 hours to overnight. Before serving, if desired, top with whole or sliced fruit or nuts of choice, or drizzle with vegan chocolate or other sauces. Serve at room temperature.

yields 6 TO 8 SERVINGS

(CONTINUES)

variations

Strawberry Cheesecake: Add ¾ cup of stemmed and diced strawberries to the cheesecake batter in the blender before blending. Decorate the top of the finished cooled cheesecake with fresh whole strawberries.

Chocolate Cheesecake: Add 6 to 8 ounces of melted and cooled vegan chocolate to the cheesecake batter in the blender before blending. You might want to cut back on the sugar, depending on how sweet the chocolate is.

Blueberry Cheesecake: Add 1 cup of fresh blueberries (or frozen, thawed) to the cheesecake batter in the blender before blending. Decorate the top of the finished cooled cheesecake with blueberries to taste.

Banana Cheesecake: Add 1½ cups of sliced very ripe bananas to the cheesecake batter in the blender before blending. You might want to cut back on the sugar.

pecan-crusted cheesecake bars

1/3 CUP VEGAN MARGARINE, AT ROOM TEMPERATURE

1/3 CUP PACKED VEGAN LIGHT BROWN SUGAR

1/3 CUP CHOPPED LIGHTLY TOASTED PECANS

1 CUP ALL-PURPOSE FLOUR

3 TABLESPOONS VEGAN GRANULATED SUGAR

8 OUNCES VEGAN CREAM CHEESE, SOFTENED (PAGE 37, OR STORE-BOUGHT)

2 TABLESPOONS SOY MILK

2 TABLESPOONS VEGAN EGG REPLACER

1 TEASPOON VANILLA EXTRACT

When you want to mix things up a little, or for more casual get-togethers such as a child's birthday party or a morning gab session with your BFF, serve these pecan-crusted cheesecake bars. They offer a deeper, more complex flavor than most other cheesecakes.

Preheat the oven to 350°F. In a standing mixer or using a handheld mixer, blend the margarine and brown sugar until fluffy. Add the pecans and flour, and stir until the mixture becomes crumbly. Set aside 1/3 cup to top the cheesecake bars.

With your fingers, press the mixture into an 8-inch square glass pan and bake for 14 minutes. Remove from the oven and let cool on a rack.

Meanwhile, make the filling: Clean the standing mixer or handheld mixer. Beat together the granulated sugar and cream cheese until very smooth. Beat in the milk, egg replacer, and vanilla, and mix well. Spread the mixture over the cooled baked crust. Sprinkle the reserved pecan mixture on top. Bake for 30 minutes. Let the cheesecake cool completely, then serve sliced into whatever size bars you wish.

yields ENOUGH TO SERVE 6 TO 8 PEOPLE DEPENDING ON THE SIZE OF THE BARS

toasted pecans

Preheat the oven to 350°F. Lightly rub a rimmed baking sheet with canola oil, wiping away excess oil with paper towels. Spread 1 cup of raw pecans on the sheet and toast them watchfully just until they release their pecan fragrance, checking after about 5 to 6 minutes. Be careful because pecans burn easily.

cheesecake party parfaits

Nostalgic, yet thoroughly hip and modern. These berry and cheesecake parfaits will bring out the child in everyone from the first spoonful onward. Tall and spectacular with layers of sliced strawberries and/or blueberries, this is about as literal as you can get in adding an exclamation point to a sensational meal with family and friends!

Preheat the oven to 350°F.

In a food processor or standing mixer, blend the tofu, cream cheese, egg replacer, sugar, and vanilla until smooth. Pour the tofu mixture into a glass baking dish and bake for about 30 minutes.

Turn off the oven, and allow the cheesecake to sit in the oven for another 40 minutes. Remove the cheesecake from the oven and allow to cool. Refrigerate for at least 4 hours or overnight.

To make the parfaits: Arrange four to six parfait glasses or wineglasses on a work surface. The number of glasses you'll need will depend on their size. Place a tablespoonful of the graham cracker crumbs in the bottom of each glass. Add a layer of berries and a layer of the cheesecake mixture. Repeat layers until the glasses are filled, ending with a cheesecake mixture layer. Garnish with a few strawberry slices and/or blueberries. Serve at once, or refrigerate for 1 to 2 hours.

yields 4 TO 6 SERVINGS

1 (14-OUNCE) PACKAGE EXTRA-FIRM SILKEN TOFU, PRESSED AND DRAINED (SEE PAGE 18)

1 CUP VEGAN CREAM CHEESE, SOFTENED (PAGE 37, OR STORE-BOUGHT)

1/4 CUP VEGAN EGG REPLACER

1/2 CUP VEGAN SUGAR

2 TEASPOONS VANILLA EXTRACT

6 TO 8 VEGAN GRAHAM CRACKERS, CRUSHED INTO LUMPY CRUMBS

15 TO 20 RIPE STRAWBERRIES, STEMMED AND SLICED, AND/OR 30 TO 40 BLUEBERRIES

note: *For best results, plan to refrigerate the cheesecake mixture overnight. If you don't have parfait glasses, use wineglasses or sleek glass bowls.*

white chocolate cheesecake petit fours

1 CUP VEGAN GRAHAM CRACKER CRUMBS

4 TABLESPOONS (½ STICK) VEGAN MARGARINE, AT ROOM TEMPERATURE

1 TABLESPOON VEGAN LIGHT BROWN SUGAR

2 CUPS VEGAN CREAM CHEESE, SOFTENED (PAGE 37, OR STORE-BOUGHT)

½ CUP VEGAN GRANULATED SUGAR

¼ CUP VEGAN EGG REPLACER

1 TEASPOON VANILLA EXTRACT, OR MORE TO TASTE

2 (24-OUNCE) PACKAGES VEGAN WHITE CHOCOLATE CHIPS

These may appear to be dainty, elegant little bonbons, but in fact these cheesecake bites topped with melted white chocolate are pretty *and* filling.

Preheat the oven to 300°F. Line a 9 by 13-inch baking dish with parchment paper.

In a medium-size bowl, mix together the graham cracker crumbs, margarine, and brown sugar until well combined. Press the crumb mixture into the bottom of the baking dish.

In a food processor, pulse the cream cheese with the granulated sugar, egg replacer, and vanilla extract until smooth. Pour the mixture into the prepared baking dish and bake until the filling has set, about 45 minutes. Remove from the heat and let cool in the pan, then refrigerate for at least 4 hours before cutting.

Cut the cheesecake into 1½- to 2-inch squares. Place in a container large enough to hold them in a single layer, cover the container, and place in the freezer until the squares are completely frozen, at least 2 hours.

In a microwave-safe bowl in a microwave oven on high, melt the white chocolate chips, stopping and stirring every 30 seconds, until the chocolate has melted and the mixture is very smooth. Let the chocolate cool for 20 minutes or so, until the chocolate is cool enough to taste with a spoon.

Remove the cheesecake from the freezer, carefully separate the squares with an offset spatula or slender knife, and place on waxed paper over a cooling rack to keep the squares cold.

With a large tablespoon, spoon the melted chocolate over the cold squares, coating all sides (except the bottoms). Refrigerate until serving time.

yields 24 PETIT FOURS

strawberry-banana cheesecake smoothie

Creamy, fruity, and delish! This blended cheesecake smoothie literally turns every lingering sip into a vacation. Feel free to add or substitute blueberries, vegan fruit preserves, or vegan chocolate syrup.

In a blender, combine all the ingredients and process until smooth. Serve immediately.

yields 1 SMOOTHIE

1 TABLESPOON VEGAN CREAM CHEESE (PAGE 37, OR STORE-BOUGHT)

½ CUP FRESH STRAWBERRIES, OR FROZEN STRAWBERRIES (THAWED), OR TO TASTE

1 RIPE BANANA

2 TABLESPOONS VEGAN GRAHAM CRACKER CRUMBS

1 CUP CRUSHED ICE

1 CUP SOY MILK, PREFERABLY VANILLA FLAVORED, OR MORE, IF DESIRED

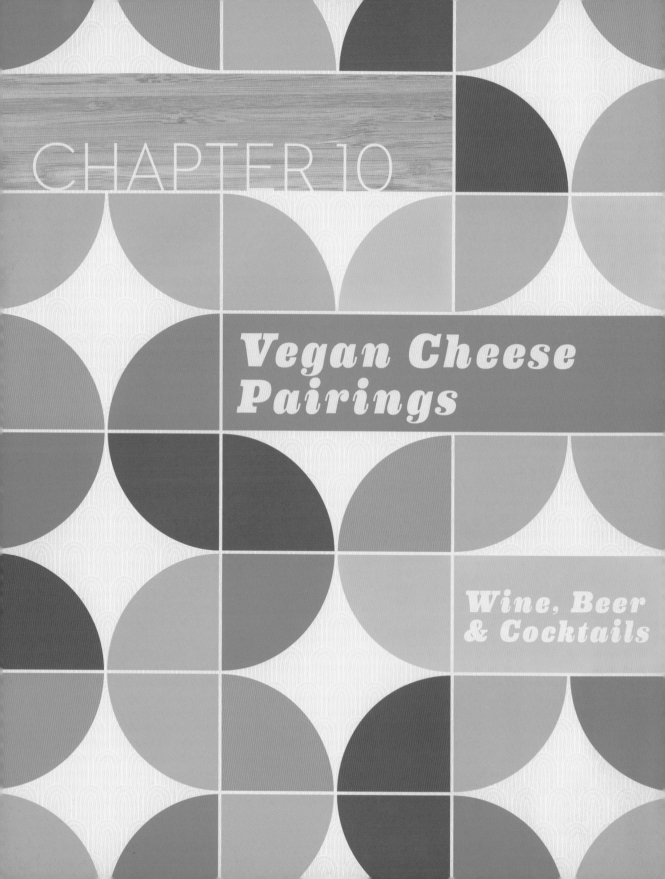

CHAPTER 10

Vegan Cheese Pairings

Wine, Beer & Cocktails

I f you think your imagination and appetite have been encouraged to run wild so far, you're about to kick it up another notch and get tipsy with it. Cheese pairings with wine, beer, and other alcohol are the ultimate chance to satisfy multiple cravings at once while taking your palate on a joyride.

Until now, vegans were left holding the bottle, *only*, at pairings. But that changes here and now! What follows is a comprehensive chart, pairing the homemade vegan cheeses from Chapter 1, and by association their related dishes throughout the book, with wines, beers, and even classic cocktails. This holds true for the store-bought variety of vegan cheeses as well.

While they are extensive in breadth, giving you as much room to play as possible, in that same spirit, I have also kept the suggestions basic, forgoing any brand names of alcohol. For example, where I suggest pairing pinot grigio or dark beer with a particular cheese, go with your favorite brand or use it as an opportunity to try a few different ones.

In addition to the pairing suggestions, in the Cheesy Vegan Table section, I lay out a variety of serving tools for all your entertaining needs. This is followed by two inventive yet easy ways to experiment and savor the cheese and spirits.

First, the fall/winter and spring/summer seasonal Vegan Artisanal Cheese Platters provide a blueprint for how you might choose appropriate cheeses for certain times of the year.

Second, I show you how you can host your very own Vegan Cheese of the Month Club or a yearlong Cheesy Vegan Pub Crawl to maximize and extend face time and a decadent happy hour with your family and friends. There aren't any rules here—mostly suggestions that you can take and explore.

american

WHITE WINE

Chardonnay

Pinot blanc

Pinot grigio

Riesling

Sauvignon blanc

Viognier

RED WINE

Beaujolais

Merlot

Pinot noir

Zinfandel (red, not too high alcohol)

BEER

Brown ale

Lager

Pilsner

COCKTAIL

Campari cocktail

Mojito

Moscow Mule (in a copper cup!)

Old Fashioned

Rusty Nail

OTHER

Bourbon

Rum

Scotch

Tequila

blue

WHITE WINE

Iced cider

Pinot grigio

Sauternes

Spatlese Riesling

Viognier

Zinfandel (white)

RED WINE

Amarone

Bordeaux (red)

Cabernet Sauvignon

Madeira

Pinot noir

Sherry (sweet)

Syrah/Shiraz

Tawny port

Zinfandel (red)

BEER

Belgian ale

English bitters

Fruit beer

IPA

Pale ale

Porter

Russian imperial stout

Stout

COCKTAIL

Vodka martini (up with unstuffed
   plain olives)

OTHER

Bourbon

Gin

Kirsch

Rye

Scotch

Tequila

Vodka

Whiskey

brie

WHITE WINE

Champagne

Chardonnay (unoaked)

Pinot blanc

Pinot grigio

Riesling

Sauvignon blanc (sparkling, Aussie)

RED WINE

Beaujolais

Bordeaux (red)

Cabernet Sauvignon

Merlot

Pinot noir

Port

Sherry (sweet)

Syrah/Shiraz

BEER

Fruit beer

Pale ale

Stout

COCKTAIL

Cosmopolitan

Vodka martini

OTHER

Bourbon

Schnapps (fruity, e.g., apple,
   peach, pear)

Tequila

Whiskey

cheddar (mild)

WHITE WINE

Cava
Champagne
Chardonnay
Pinot blanc
Pinot grigio

RED WINE

Beaujolais
Cabernet Sauvignon
Merlot
Pinot noir

BEER

Lager
Pilsner

COCKTAIL

Gin martini
Old Fashioned

OTHER

Bourbon
Brandy
Cognac
Irish whiskey (on the rocks)
Rum
Scotch

cheddar (sharp)

WHITE WINE

Champagne
Crémant
Franciacorta
Pinot grigio
Riesling
Sake
Sauvignon blanc

RED WINE

Cabernet Sauvignon
Chianti
Merlot
Pinot noir (California or Burgundy)
Rioja
Syrah/Shiraz
Zinfandel (red)

BEER

Belgian ale
Bock
Brown ale
Fruit beer
Pale ale
Porter
Stout
Wheat Beer

COCKTAIL

Gin martini
Irish whiskey (on the rocks)
Old Fashioned

OTHER

Bourbon
Brandy
Cognac
Gin
Rum
Scotch

cottage cheese

WHITE WINE

Sauvignon blanc

BEER

Pale ale

COCKTAIL

Mint Julep (in a silver cup!)
Stinger

OTHER

Amaretto
Bourbon whiskey

cream cheese

WHITE WINE

Champagne
Chardonnay
Pinot blanc
Pinot grigio
Sauvignon blanc
Viognier
Zinfandel (white)

RED WINE

Beaujolais nouveau
Chianti
Merlot
Pinot Noir

BEER

Fruit beer
Lager
Red ale

COCKTAIL

Bloody Mary

OTHER

Canadian whiskey
Scotch

feta

WHITE WINE

Champagne
Chardonnay
Chenin blanc
Pinot blanc
Pinot grigio
Pouilly-Fumé
Riesling
Sauvignon blanc
Viognier

RED WINE

Beaujolais
Pinot noir

BEER

Fruit beer
Lager
Pilsner
Wheat beer

COCKTAIL

Sidecar

OTHER

Ouzo
Schnapps (fruity, e.g., apple,
    peach, pear)

horseradish cheese

*(american and cheddar
variations)*

WINE

Pinot blanc
Pinot grigio
Riesling (high acidity)

BEER

Fruit beer
Wheat beer

COCKTAIL

Bloody Mary
Rum & Coke

OTHER

Gin
Vodka

jack

WHITE WINE

Chardonnay

Pinot blanc

Pinot grigio

Riesling

Sauvignon blanc

Viognier

RED WINE

Beaujolais

Merlot

Pinot noir

Zinfandel (red, not too high alcohol)

BEER

Brown ale

Lager

Pilsner

COCKTAIL

Bloody Mary

Whiskey Sour

OTHER

Rum

Tequila

Vodka

mozzarella

WHITE WINE

Champagne

Chardonnay

Pinot blanc

Pinot grigio

Sauvignon blanc

Viognier

RED WINE

Beaujolais

Chianti

Merlot

Pinot noir

Sangiovese

BEER

Fruit beer

Pilsner

Wheat beer

COCKTAIL

Campari cocktail

OTHER

Sambuca

Vodka

muenster

WHITE WINE

Chardonnay

Gewürztraminer

Gruner Veltliner

Pinot blanc

Pinot grigio

Riesling

Sauvignon blanc

Zinfandel (white)

RED WINE

Beaujolais

Merlot

Pinot noir

Zinfandel (red)

BEER

Belgian ale

Lager

Pale ale

Pilsner

Porter

Stout

COCKTAIL

Daiquiri

El Presidente

Old Fashioned

OTHER

Bourbon

Brandy

nooch cheese

WHITE WINE

Cava
Champagne
Chardonnay
Pinot blanc
Pinot grigio

RED WINE

Beaujolais
Merlot
Pinot noir

BEER

Lager
Pilsner

COCKTAIL

Gin Sling
Margarita

OTHER

Bourbon
Brandy
Cognac
Rum
Scotch
Whiskey

parmesan

WHITE WINE

Champagne
Chardonnay
Pinot grigio
Riesling
Sake
Sauvignon blanc

RED WINE

Amarone
Cabernet Sauvignon
Chianti
Merlot
Ripasso
Sangiovese
Syrah/Shiraz
Zinfandel (red)

BEER

Amber ale
Amber lager
Pale ale
Pilsner
Stout

COCKTAIL

Bellini

OTHER

Brandy
Scotch
Vodka

ricotta

WHITE WINE

Chardonnay
Pinot blanc
Pinot grigio
Viognier

RED WINE

Cabernet Sauvignon (young)
Chianti
Sangiovese

BEER

Lager
Pale ale
Pilsner

COCKTAIL

Dirty Martini
Tom Collins

OTHER

Brandy
Gin

smoked cheese
(cheddar, cream cheese, and mozzarella variations)

WHITE WINE

Chardonnay

RED WINE

Merlot

Rioja

BEER

Beer, beer, beer! of choice

Rauchbier

Smoked porter

COCKTAIL

Manhattan

Rob Roy

OTHER

Brandy

Vermouth (sweet)

Whiskey

swiss

WHITE WINE

Asti

Champagne

Chardonnay

Gewürztraminer

Pinot grigio

Riesling

Sauvignon blanc

RED WINE

Beaujolais

Bonarda

Cabernet Sauvignon

Merlot

Pinotage

Pinot noir

BEER

Bock

Lager (preferably dark)

Pale ale

Wheat beer

COCKTAIL

Black Russian

Manhattan

OTHER

Vermouth (sweet)

Vodka

Whiskey

wine cheese

WINE

Serve with wine used in the cheese

BEER

Amber lager

Dark beer

the cheesy vegan table

Whether sneaking a chunk of cheese to hold you over until suppertime or putting on a dinner party, pairing, or larger bash, every bite is meant to be savored with efficiency and style. No matter the occasion, following are some essential serving tools that will leave no doubt in anyone's mind who is the cheesiest vegan host or hostess around.

The homemade vegan cheese recipes in Chapter 1 give us all a reason to either use grandma's heirloom cheese board and dome for their intended purposes or to go shopping for some fun and even artistic-looking cheese tools to add to our kitchen collections. While the following items are easily found in mainstream stores, specialty shops, and even antique stores, for a guide to online resources offering chef-grade and even whimsical tools, see the Resource Guide for Cheese Tools on page 234.

SLICERS

When it comes to cheese, a simple knife alone usually doesn't cut it (literally). The last thing you want to serve yourself or guests is a ragged, uneven slice of cheese. Traditional slicers come in many shapes and sizes. Depending on your specific needs, it is best to go with a stainless-steel plane slicer, wire slicer, or specific cheese/chef's all-purpose utility knife that will insure safe, clean, and uniform slices for sandwiches or for serving alone with crackers.

If serving multiple cheeses at a party or tasting where guests will cut their own slices, use a separate knife for each cheese to avoid mixing the flavors.

GRATERS

Cheese graters give you a lot of bang for your buck. They also multitask as graters for chocolate, vegetables, and more. Choose a stainless-steel grater with a firm grip and razor-sharp blades to ensure perfectly grated cheese to use as an ingredient or as a colorful topping for salads, soups, and more. Box graters are also available, usually with catch basins, but with these, be careful that cheese is the only thing being grated, and not your knuckles (i.e., keep your eyes on the prize)! Some deluxe graters offer different-size grating options, along with a slicer.

PLATTERS

When it comes to a serving vessel, there are a few things to keep in mind. It's best if the surface is flat, so that if you're serving multiple cheeses together they won't run together. Consider offering each cheese on its own small platter, which totally prevents the cheeses' running together and their aromas' intermingling.

As for the platter itself, a wooden cutting board will forever be the benchmark for serving cheese. These days, wooden serving boards are not limited to round, square, and rectangular but come in many shapes and sizes, even thematic designs, such as pianos, guitars, wine bottles, animals, and more. Other traditional cheese platters are also available in glass and marble.

DOMES

New or antique, a clear glass cheese dome is one of the most charming accents in a kitchen. Inducing an instantly cozy mood, cheese domes are practical in keeping cheese from drying too much while sitting out, and aesthetically they create an instant focal point for any get-together. In addition to providing a stage for your vegan cheese to shine, domes can also be used in conjunction with serving boards, plates, or pedestals to display cookies, candies, cakes, fruit, and more. If serving more than one cheese, consider using multiple plates and pedestals to create varying levels, all covered with a collection of differently shaped domes.

CHEESE LABELS

For all those boozy cheese pairings, it's all about the details when it comes to impressing your guests. There are such things as cheese-serving labels. Made of porcelain or other materials onto which you can handwrite a cheese's moniker, they serve as decorative nameplates for your guests' convenience when inserted into each cheese you're offering.

CHEESE TOTES

Major Gift Alert for all the cheese lovers in your life . . . starting with you! When you want to take your Cheesy Vegan show on the road for picnics, beach adventures, campouts, and backyard parties, there are specially designed and insulated totes that have compartments for everything you'll need, from the slicers and cutting board to the cheese and wine/beer/beverages of choice. Often, the totes already come with the tools. Smaller travel kits with only the tools are also available.

ACCESSORIES

We've all seen them; some of us (not naming names) may have even donned one from time to time when cheering on a favorite sports team or indulging a silly mood. But now, we can all wear one in celebration of this new era of cheese for all. Yep, I'm talking Cheeseheads!

When the mood strikes you, the original source for the classic Cheesehead hat, which comes in adult, youth, and even . . . *Wait. For. It.* . . . doll sizes for the whole family to enjoy, is Foamation (Cheesehead .com). For the cheesy fashionistas out there, or as playful host and hostess gifts, be sure to also check out the Cheesehead fedora, top hat, cowboy hat, bow tie, necktie, earrings, pins, belt buckle, earmuffs, and so much more.

artisanal vegan cheese platters by the season

While dishes loaded with cheese as an ingredient are always a crowd-pleaser, nothing revs up the eyes and palate like a platter (or collection of separate serving vessels) brimming with different cheeses and crackers, accompanied by the appropriate fruits and vegetables.

Following are suggestions for cheeses, in slices, cubes, and spreads per your preference, to create artisanal vegan cheese platters for fall/winter and spring/summer. These ideas are followed by a list of fruits and vegetables to dress up the platters in appropriate bite-size pieces. These colorful platters can stand alone as solo party or snack fare, or be served as appetizers or a first course, or even as an alternative dessert course.

Naturally, the appropriate (or your favorite) wine, beer, and cocktail pairings will always be a winning and welcome combo. For pairing suggestions, refer back to the chart at the beginning of this chapter.

THE FALL/WINTER VEGAN ARTISANAL CHEESE PLATTER

This is the cozy, fireplace-crackling time of the year when heavier and richer cheeses and flavors are most welcome. Along with the fruits and vegetables of choice (see list on page 229), serve the cheeses with a selection of crackers and vegan mustards.

On a platter or series of separate serving plates, arrange slices, cubes, or spreads of the following homemade cheeses from Chapter 1:

- Extra-sharp Cheddar (page 28)
- Smoked Cheddar (page 28)
- Horseradish Cheddar (page 28)
- Wine (page 30)
- Smoked Mozzarella (page 31)
- Swiss (page 34)
- Brie (page 33)

- Horseradish American (page 45)
- Cream Cheese (using the 'Tis the Season Fruit & Nut Ball [page 158] or Pecan & Cranberry Party Log [page 161])

THE SPRING/SUMMER VEGAN ARTISANAL CHEESE PLATTER

At this carefree time of the year when nearly everything is in full bloom, you're going to want lighter cheeses and flavors. Along with the fruits and vegetables of choice (see list on this page), serve the cheeses with a selection of crackers and vegan mustards.

On a platter or series of separate serving plates, arrange slices, cubes, or spreads of the following homemade cheeses from Chapter 1:

- Cheddar (page 28)
- Mozzarella (page 31)
- Jack (page 42)
- Blue (page 41)
- Muenster (page 44)
- American (page 45)
- Cream cheese (page 37, using one or more of the garlic, jalapeño, farmers' market veggie, hot sauce, and smoked variations)

Fruits & Vegetables

Whether from your backyard or local farmers' market, or some other source, choose fruits and vegetables that speak to you. Use those that you think will best complement the colors and flavors of the cheeses you're using and the wine, beer, and cocktails you're serving. This is by no means a scientific equation, so don't overthink it. This is about experimenting, learning how new and seasonal flavors mix and match, and, most of all, having a fun time.

Accompany the cheese slices, cubes, and spreads with a selection of the following fruits and vegetables, or any others you would like to use:

Fruits:
- Apple wedges
- Pear slices
- Grape clusters
- Cantaloupe slices
- Peach slices
- Strawberries
- Papaya slices
- Kiwi slices
- Olives (such as pitted kalamatas and pitted jumbo green olives, as well as Fried Olives Stuffed with Smoky Cheese Hummus [page 150] and Casanova's Blue Cheese- or Feta-Stuffed Cocktail Olives [page 153])

Vegetables:
- Tomato wedges or cherry tomatoes
- Red or yellow bell pepper slices
- Green onions
- Cucumber slices
- Carrot sticks
- Asparagus spears (raw or olive-oiled, roasted, and cooled)
- Cauliflower florets (raw or olive-oiled, roasted, and cooled)
- Broccoli florets (raw or olive-oiled, roasted, and cooled)

vegan cheese of the month club

When I cohosted a yearlong charity pub crawl with my family's brewery, the biggest lesson I learned was: You don't need to have all the fun at once. The same goes for cheese. Whereas the artisanal vegan cheese platters offer the indulgence of one-stop shopping by the season, another equally gratifying option is to focus on one cheese every month.

To launch your own Vegan Cheese of the Month Club: Each month, choose a vegan cheese from Chapter 1 to make (or opt for a store-bought brand if you prefer; see the Store-Bought Vegan Cheese Resource Guide on page 233). Pair the cheese with the appropriate wines, beers, and cocktails (see the pairing chart on page 220), and send out the invites. You can even accompany the sliced, cubed, or spreadable cheesy happy hour with a round of appetizers and snacks from Chapter 6 and/or a lunch or dinner course featuring a dish prepared with the spotlighted cheese of the month.

In fact, you and your friends can divide and conquer by each of you choosing a month and hosting your own pairing for a true yearlong Cheesy Vegan Pub Crawl.

And keep in mind that homemade vegan cheese makes a unique host or hostess gift, or an anytime present for all the cheese lovers in your life. And that would be pretty much everyone, right?

The following is a suggested Vegan Cheese of the Month Club schedule to get you started. But please feel free to mix it up and run off on as many cheesy and tipsy tangents as you'd like, to make this twelve-month vegan cheese extravaganza rock the loudest (and tastiest) for you and your friends.

- **January:** Swiss (page 34)
- **February:** Cheddar (page 28) and/or Smoked Cheddar (page 28)
- **March:** Muenster (page 44)
- **April:** Blue (page 41)
- **May:** Mozzarella (page 31)
- **June:** Jack (page 42)
- **July:** American (page 45)
- **August:** Cream cheese (page 37, using one or more of the garlic, jalapeño, farmers' market veggie, hot sauce, and smoked variations)
- **September:** Wine cheese (page 30)
- **October:** Smoked Mozzarella (page 31)
- **November:** Horseradish American (page 45) and/or Horseradish Cheddar (page 28)
- **December:** Brie (page 33) and/or 'Tis the Season Fruit & Nut Ball (page 158)

metric conversions

- The recipes in this book have not been tested with metric measurements, so some variations might occur.

- Remember that the weight of dry ingredients varies according to the volume or density factor: 1 cup of flour weighs far less than 1 cup of sugar, and 1 tablespoon doesn't necessarily hold 3 teaspoons.

GENERAL FORMULA FOR METRIC CONVERSION

Ounces to grams	ounces × 28.35 = grams
Grams to ounces	grams × 0.035 = ounces
Pounds to grams	pounds × 453.5 = grams
Pounds to kilograms	pounds × 0.45 = kilograms
Cups to liters	cups × 0.24 = liters
Fahrenheit to Celsius	(°F – 32) × 5 ÷ 9 = °C
Celsius to Fahrenheit	(°C × 9) ÷ 5 + 32 = °F

VOLUME (LIQUID) MEASUREMENTS

1 teaspoon = $^1/_6$ fluid ounce = 5 milliliters

1 tablespoon = $^1/_2$ fluid ounce = 15 milliliters

2 tablespoons = 1 fluid ounce = 30 milliliters

$^1/_4$ cup = 2 fluid ounces = 60 milliliters

$^1/_3$ cup = $2^2/_3$ fluid ounces = 79 milliliters

$^1/_2$ cup = 4 fluid ounces = 118 milliliters

1 cup or $^1/_2$ pint = 8 fluid ounces = 250 milliliters

2 cups or 1 pint = 16 fluid ounces = 500 milliliters

4 cups or 1 quart = 32 fluid ounces = 1,000 milliliters

1 gallon = 4 liters

VOLUME (DRY) MEASUREMENTS

$^1/_4$ teaspoon = 1 milliliter

$^1/_2$ teaspoon = 2 milliliters

$^3/_4$ teaspoon = 4 milliliters

1 teaspoon = 5 milliliters

1 tablespoon = 15 milliliters

$^1/_4$ cup = 59 milliliters

$^1/_3$ cup = 79 milliliters

$^1/_2$ cup = 118 milliliters

$^2/_3$ cup = 158 milliliters

$^3/_4$ cup = 177 milliliters

1 cup = 225 milliliters

4 cups or 1 quart = 1 liter

$^1/_2$ gallon = 2 liters

1 gallon = 4 liters

OVEN TEMPERATURE EQUIVALENTS, FAHRENHEIT (F) AND CELSIUS (C)

100°F = 38°C

200°F = 95°C

250°F = 120°C

300°F = 150°C

350°F = 180°C

400°F = 205°C

450°F = 230° C

WEIGHT (MASS) MEASUREMENTS

1 ounce = 30 grams

2 ounces = 55 grams

3 ounces = 85 grams

4 ounces = $^1/_4$ pound = 125 grams

8 ounces = $^1/_2$ pound = 240 grams

12 ounces = $^3/_4$ pound = 375 grams

16 ounces = 1 pound = 454 grams

LINEAR MEASUREMENTS

$^1/_2$ in = $1^1/_2$ cm

1 inch = $2^1/_2$ cm

6 inches = 15 cm

8 inches = 20 cm

10 inches = 25 cm

12 inches = 30 cm

20 inches = 50 cm

store-bought vegan cheese resource guide

In addition to using the homemade vegan cheeses from Chapter 1 in the recipes and pairings throughout this book, you can also use the vegan cheeses produced by the following companies. These cheeses are becoming more widely available in grocery stores and online.

Bute Island Foods Ltd
www.buteisland.com

Chicago Vegan Foods
www.chicagoveganfoods.com

Daiya Foods
www.daiyafoods.com

Dixie Diners' Club
www.dixiediner.com

Dr-Cow
www.dr-cow.com

Edward & Sons (Road's End Organics)
www.edwardandsons.com

Fat Goblin (Nacho Mom's)
www.fatgoblin.com

Follow Your Heart
www.followyourheart.com

Galaxy Nutritional Foods
www.galaxyfoods.com

Heidi Ho Veganics
www.heidihoveganics.com

Lisanatti Foods
www.lisanatti.com

Punk Rawk Labs
www.punkrawklabs.net

Ste Martaen
www.stemartaen.com

Sister River Foods
www.eatparma.com

The Redwood Whole Food Company
www.shop.redwoodfoods.eu

Tofutti
www.tofutti.com

index

Avocado & Parmesan Pita Lunch Rush, page 124 ▶

Flying Buffalo Pizza, page 177 ▶